Pixel Art

for

Game Developers

Pixel Art

for

Game Developers

//by
//Daniel Silber

CRC Press
Taylor & Francis Group
Boca Raton London New York

CRC Press is an imprint of the
Taylor & Francis Group, an **informa** business

AN A K PETERS BOOK

CRC Press
Taylor & Francis Group
6000 Broken Sound Parkway NW, Suite 300
Boca Raton, FL 33487-2742

First issued in hardback 2017

© 2016 by Taylor & Francis Group, LLC
CRC Press is an imprint of Taylor & Francis Group, an Informa business

No claim to original U.S. Government works

ISBN 13: 978-1-138-41355-9 (hbk)
ISBN 13: 978-1-4822-5230-9 (pbk)

Visit the Taylor & Francis Web site at
http://www.taylorandfrancis.com

and the CRC Press Web site at
http://www.crcpress.com

Contents

Preface: What the Crap Is Pixel Art?

As a kid, did you ever get right up close to the TV despite your parents' warnings that it will make you cross-eyed and turn your eyes into bloody stumps? If you did, you would have noticed that the images were created with tiny dots of bright color. Those tiny dots are called pixels. Pixels compose the images that are displayed on TVs, computer monitors, tablets, phones, and most other digital devices.

Computer graphics were originally built by manipulating those dots of color one pixel at a time, which became the early history of Pixel Art. In some cases, those pixels were controlled through cumbersome programming scripts but over time computer art programs became more common and the quality of representation improved.

Pixel Art grew out of technical restraints from a generation ago. Game systems had much less memory and worked with much smaller pixel dimensions than today, so it was a technical necessity to work within tight restraints on size and color.

As games grew in quality and sophistication, it became important to make the most out of the aesthetics within the technical restraints. Out of this era, some "best practices" grew out of the process and have evolved into what we now think of as Pixel Art.

Before starting to rant on the many useful aspects of Pixel Art in games and applications or even explaining what Pixel Art is, I want to give examples of what it is not.

3D graphics are not Pixel Art (Figure F.1), despite that they are being created by pixels on screen.

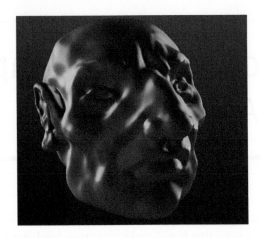

FIGURE F.1   3D graphics are not Pixel Art.

Vector graphics (Figure F.2), the type commonly built in Adobe Illustrator or Adobe Flash, are not Pixel Art.

FIGURE F.2   This is vector art, not Pixel Art.

FIGURE F.3   Also vector art.

FIGURE F.4   Yet more vector art.

Vector graphics (Figures F.3 and F.4) are built by laying out points (called vectors) and the shape of curves that create the lines that connect those curves (called the speed of the curve). Then gradients can be generated to fill in those lines. It is a lovely style but built with a methodology markedly different from Pixel Art.

Traditional art that has been scanned into the computer is not Pixel Art, despite that it is now visible by the use of pixels on screen. This would now be considered a bitmapped graphic (Figure F.5). Even when reduced to very small pixel dimensions, as done in Figure F.6, this would not be considered Pixel Art. Although once reduced, we are getting a little bit closer.

FIGURE F.5   Hand-drawn art scanned into the computer are considered bitmapped art.

FIGURE F.6   Bitmaps that have been reduced are still not Pixel Art.

Also of note is that not all 2D art that was painted on the computer is considered Pixel Art. A painting created in Photoshop or Corel does not usually fall into this category either. Take a look at Figure F.7, and you can see that although this piece was clearly built in the computer, the individual pixels are not really visible without looking very closely.

FIGURE F.7   Still not Pixel Art.

I'll now define specifically what I mean by "Pixel Art."

Pixel Art: An image where each pixel visible on screen is placed intentionally.

Fortunately for us, this does not mean that every pixel has to be placed by hand. Large areas of the same color can be filled in with a "fill" tool, and a "line" tool can place dozens of pixels at once. The important thing is that each pixel that shows up on screen was intended to be where it is.

Some examples are shown in Figures F.8 and F.9.

FIGURE F.8   Screenshot from Pixel Guy's Quest. This is Pixel Art.

FIGURE F.9   Another example of Pixel Art.

It may sound tedious, but there are many tools and methods we can use to make the process fast and easy—and fun! And as you can see from the examples, there is plenty of opportunity for detail using this suite of techniques.

Acknowledgments

WHEN I SET OUT TO CREATE THIS BOOK by writing bits and pieces in my kitchen, I had the very false expectation of being a lone wolf—putting together the various parts in isolation. As it turned out, this was not at all the case and the book could not have come together without the help and guidance of many incredible people.

This book would have suffered in quality (if it was finished at all) without the assistance of these wonderful people. I relied heavily on these folks in entirely unexpected ways.

First and foremost, I'd like to give a huge, gigantic thank-you to my publisher and editor. You are the best and I intend to buy you cocktails whenever I see you next!

Rick Adams—executive editor at CRC Press

Joselyn Banks—project coordinator and editor on my project from CRC Press

Suzanne Lassandro—project editor at CRC Press

Scott Hayes—prepress manager at CRC Press

Rick was extremely patient with me and managed to talk to me kindly even when I was at my most anxious. Josie, thank you for taking my ugly manuscript and turning it into this amazing final product!

I would like to express my appreciation to the initial reviewers of the book whose input early on in the process was invaluable:

Chris Totten—professor of game design at American University

Chris Kaplan—senior multimedia developer at GP Strategies Corporation

Callen Shaw—CEO at The Unallied

Special thanks to the incredibly talented developers that contributed to the book:

James Petruzzi and the fine folks at Discord games

Jochum Skoglund and Niklas Myrberg of Crackshell games

Alex Preston of Heart Machine

The input given by the following people was greatly appreciated and went a long way toward helping to give birth to the final product:

Josh Jennings—game developer and artist

Francis Coloumbe—Pixel Art guru

My wonderful family—the coolest people I know!

I would also like to extend my thanks to Ron Cyran, who tolerated my wonky work schedule throughout this crazy process. Although listed earlier, I want to give a special nod of appreciation to Professor Chris Totten. This book would likely never have been written without his contributions.

CHAPTER 1

Why Pixel Art?

Now you know what we're talking about when we say Pixel Art, but why would we use something that grew out of *technical restraints*?

There are a lot of motives for using Pixel Art, but we can basically break them into two primary categories: the reasons that have to do with the players' enjoyment and the jubilant blissful euphoria of the developer that uses this methodology.

1.1 PLAYERS LOVE PIXEL ART

The Pixel Art aesthetic is loved and revered by many players, and there are some very good reasons! The style triggers warm feeling of nostalgia for many of us older gamers, yet is contemporary and found in some of the best games made today. There is something about the simplicity of the style that lends itself to memorable and iconic imagery. Let's take a moment to discuss why players are so drawn to Pixel Art.

1.1.1 Sweet Nostalgia

The most obvious way that Pixel Art connects with audiences is through its connection to earlier times in video/computer gaming history.

The kids who grew up playing games in the 1980s and 1990s have an intrinsic affinity for this aesthetic. For many in this generation, the style taps into warm feelings of nostalgia. When I play a game with tight Pixel Art, it unconsciously tickles memories of being nine years old and trading Nintendo cartridges with friends. For me personally, the look brings me back to a simpler time…A time before getting beaten up by a bunch of members of the Cobra Kai dressed in skeleton costumes.

1.1.2 Contemporary and Relevant

This generation has seen game genres fracture into more and more different types of experiences. Today we have computer games ranging from FPS to RPS to MMOs, mobile games from casual to tactical, F2P, subscription based, art games, experimental games, arcade games, console games, downloadable content, and dozens of other genres and subgenres. There are more types of experiences available than ever before, and equally numerous aesthetics.

There have become a great many acceptable styles throughout the various categories, and it appears that Pixel Art has remained strong through the test of time.

In recent years (at the time this book is written), there have been far too many games using Pixel Art to list them all, but here is a list of some of the highlights of current gen games either built or being built with Pixel Art (Figures 1.1 and 1.2):

Chasm by Discord Games

Superbrothers: Sword and Sworcery EP by Capybara Games

Super Dwarf Madness by The Unallied

Super Crate Box by Vlambeer

Tiny Barbarian by StarQuail

Crawl by Powerhoof

Shovel Knight by Yacht Club Games

FIGURE 1.1   Screenshot from Chasm.

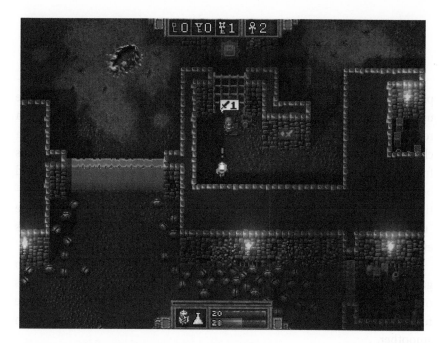

FIGURE 1.2   Screenshot from Hammerwatch.

And there are, honestly, so many other quality games built in this style that I wouldn't ever try to create a comprehensive list. I couldn't possibly manage to list them all!

1.1.3 Pixel Art Is Iconic

Because Pixel Art is created from little squares and genuine curves are not available, it lends itself to exaggeration. Features become somewhat iconic versions of whatever they are intended to represent, which can be surprisingly useful.

Pixel Art is a clearly stylized representation, and it is easy to use this aspect to your advantage. The Mario character that we all know and love was built as an exaggeration of a nose and mustache simply to make the character stand out. Shigeru Miyamoto explains in an interview with *Popular Mechanics* from December of 2009:

> With the technology back then, you had very limited palette in which you were able to draw a character. If you look at the original Mario face, you had just 7 pixels to draw his face. My goal within that limited palette was to create a character that

was as distinct as possible. Because of that, he had some of his now-distinct features such as his big nose.*

Another wonderful aspect overlooked by most is that you almost completely circumvent the "uncanny valley" by using this simplified style. The uncanny valley is the concept that as characters look more and more like a real human they look more appealing—with one very large exception. If a character looks almost human but not exactly—if there are small deviations from reality—the character looks "uncanny." Some examples of this would be wax dummies, some humanoid robots, and 3D characters where animation makes their joint movement appear unnatural. The effect is called the "uncanny valley" because of the dip in the graph that is used to show this effect.

Good Pixel Art looks intentional and timeless. The quality 2D video games of the 1990s can stand side by side with the quality Pixel Art games of today. So Pixel Art is well received by many audiences, but the more fundamental truth is that it can make your development process much smoother.

1.2 IT MAKES YOUR LIFE EASIER

So Pixel Art may be considered an "acceptable style" to players…But why would you want use Pixel Art?

1.2.1 Smaller File Sizes

I wanted to start with the most measurable and pragmatic fact: the file sizes for Pixel Art can be extremely small. Using a tiled background thoughtfully, it would be quite feasible to have the background data for an entire game fit on one 640×480 image with a reasonable amount of variation. It's not that this would always be the best choice, but that it is possible to work within that restraint and still have a quality product is somewhat amazing.

This also gives the opportunity to have more objects on screen without performance issues. Of course, that aspect is somewhat hindered if there are a lot of semitransparent parts of each sprite. That means that you can fit more content into a single game.

---

* Popular Mechanics, New York. http://www.popularmechanics.com/technology/gadgets/video-games/4334387.

Another more subtle luxury that small file sizes create is that the game will compile faster. As those of you from the programming discipline know, a slow compile can be a huge lag on development time and somewhat maddening for the developer. You'll be loving life with your speedy compile times!

1.2.2 *Anyone* Can Create Pixel Art

This may be an exaggeration, as there, very well, may be people who would not be able to create Pixel Art…Blind people, perhaps someone with no arms or legs…But in most cases people can learn to become reasonably skilled with the medium if they choose. That is a big advantage of using Pixel Art—it is very accessible as a development tool. It's easy to learn, the software is cheap, and it's easy to integrate into games.

Almost anyone can learn to create Pixel Art, and, what's more, the process is fun! The relative simplicity of the style heavily limits the amount of work that is needed to create production quality artwork. This dramatically lowers the bar to entry to the graphics side of game development.

What's more, once the basics have been learned, you can gradually add small bits of detail to your scenes—which have the potential to make the final outcome of your effort rather dazzling. Although the individual parts are simple, Pixel Art can be layered, which can become quite complex and visually stunning.

It's also a good option for your wallet, as there are many good software packages available for free or cheap. My favorite Pixel Art program at the moment is a program called Cosmigo Pro Motion. At the time of the writing of this book, it costs roughly $100. There are many tools within the program such as a tile environment editor that makes it an excellent investment if you want to excel with this skill. And so far as I can tell, that is the upper-end price for Pixel Art software! There are in fact many other great programs that are available for free or for cheap online.

The relative price of the software, the painless learning curve, as well as the general ease of creation and integration with code all make it a super accessible development tool.

1.2.3 Spend Less Time Doing Boring Stuff

Not only is it easy to create, but it is easy to work with too! When done properly, the files sizes are almost comically small. This makes all of the file management very fast and easy. The small file sizes make the work fast and easy to import into game engines…And as mentioned earlier, the compile times for games of this ilk become very short (unless a large amount of music is slowing down the process).

Having smaller file sizes means the game will download faster, making for much easier file management. What's more, the fast download time will improve the game experience for the player.

In most cases the finished art can be exported in many different formats: png, gif, spr, etc. Since image files are so common, almost any engine or programming language will be able to make use of the art assets.

1.2.4 It Works Well on Very Small Screens

Because each pixel is in its place, it lends itself to very small resolutions. The term resolution refers to the actual number of pixels that a particular screen has to display an image and is usually written as width × height like this: 720 × 480 (which incidentally is one of the standard DVD resolutions). Most HD televisions are either 1280 × 720 (720p) or 1920 × 1080 (1080p)…But many phones and mobile devices commonly have a resolution much smaller. Consider the Nintendo DS, where each screen has a resolution of 256 × 192—that poses a substantial difference in the way that the image is interpreted by your eyes.

When working with other sorts of graphics, the final output of the image is still created with pixels. This is relevant because whenever an image is reduced to a smaller size, the final outcome will only have the available resolution to "draw" the image. To give an example, Figure 1.3 is a painting that was scanned in at 1756 × 2259. Looks pretty good, but let's say you want this as a sprite in your game—when we drop this guy down to a resolution of 75 × 97 (a decently large size for most sprites in a 2D game), then we get the abomination seen in Figure 1.4.

FIGURE 1.3   A scanned image at
1756 × 2259 pixel resolution.

FIGURE 1.4   The same image reduced
to a 75 × 97 pixel resolution.

1.2.5 Pixel Art: It's Better than 3D

I didn't mean it! Call off the threatening goons—I love 3D art also! I'm talking only of ease of the creation pipeline.

In truth, many people are surprised when I tell them that the ability to place pixels aesthetically is actually one of the most useful skills to have in development today. For some reason when people think of games they immediately think of complicated 3D graphics and seem surprised when told that there are thousands of current generation games being made with Pixel Art.

So let's take a moment and compare the workflow of creating a character animation in 3D against building the same game asset as Pixel Art.

Building a character animation using 3D technology:

- Model the character

- Lay out the UVs

- Create a texture

- Create a zBrush, mudbox, etc., hi-poly version and create normal maps

- Create a skeleton and setup a rig

- Skin the character and paint UV weights

- Create animation

- Import all assets (model, animations, textures, etc.) into the game environment

- Make sure that the model, texture(s), and animations link up properly within the game engine

Building a character animation using Pixel Art

- Create character animation

- Import into game engine

You can easily see the advantage of a shorter pipeline method. Of course, neither is really "better" any more than screwdriver is better than a hammer—I'm just being a rabble-rouser to make sure you haven't entirely fallen asleep. It's obvious that these are simply different tools that can be used in different contexts.

But it may be fair to say that, on the whole, Pixel Art is usually far faster, less expensive, and more reliable than building in 3D.

1.2.6 All Your Friends Are Doing It and It'll Make You Cool

It's hip to be square (I am so sorry for that pun). The pixel aesthetic has a retro chic feel and a huge following throughout the game-playing community. And it's free the first time too!

In truth, there are some great communities online where people chat and give critique on each other's work. I'm a member of several forums and they have all been super welcoming and helpful.

In a world where smartphones have become commonplace, working within tight visual constraints has become a utilitarian skill. The aesthetic is widely used in games today—players love it because of the nostalgia as well as it's iconic nature.

There are so many ways in which this style is practical and functional to developers like you. The small file sizes, accessibility, pipeline, and awesome community make it a super fun way to create art for your game.

CHAPTER 2

Pixel Art

The Technology of Yesterday...Today!

2.1 WHY NOW? WHAT'S IN IT FOR YOU?

Pixel Art has been around a long time—more than 30 years. Why would anybody want to use such an antiquated style?

We just talked about a lot of the value in creating your games using this style... But don't feel bound by all of the utility that Pixel Art offers. You may just like the look of Pixel Art and simply want me to validate the purchase, but in this book you will learn a solid foundation for building graphics.

This book will teach you how to create Pixel Art with a particular focus on creating art assets to be used in video games. You can expect to learn how to create professional quality imagery within the constraints that guide software development.

Specifically, you will learn:

- The principles of drawing with pixels

- How to effectively use color palettes

- To create and use tiled backgrounds

- The essentials of building for speed and consistency

- Introduction to animating with pixels

- To build graphics that will meet a game's technical requirements

- How to connect with game developers who need Pixel Art

Throughout this book there are tutorials to give you experience applying the various principles discussed, with screenshots to document the steps of the creation process.

2.2 WHO THIS BOOK IS FOR

Artists, programmers, hobbyists, and indie developers. If you've picked up the book in curiosity, it's probably for *you*.

2.2.1 Artists

You already know how to make things look good, so you have a natural advantage in *some* aspects of Pixel Art creation. I say only some aspects because a large part of working with pixels has to do with trading off realism for efficiency and that can be a difficult choice for some artists (myself included).

This book will help you to systematize your process so that the work will flow out faster and with more consistency. There are also idiosyncrasies that are unique to this medium, with useful tricks to help you make top quality work. I wish to also make you aware of potential pitfalls and what you can do to circumvent those problems.

For some this may bridge the gap between being able to draw and having the skills to landing a job within the game industry (which can be notoriously difficult to break in to).

2.2.2 Programmers (Fire Your Artist and Do It Yourself)

Pixel Art at its finest borrows many concepts from programming: reuse, inherence, and dynamic information—just to name a few.

After reading and completing the exercises in this book, you should fully understand the process necessary to build production-quality work. You may find yourself more at home within this medium that you expect.

Even if you continue to outsource your art production, this will give you a deeper understanding of the process—giving you tools to communicate your needs more effectively, saving you effort (and money!) In truth there is a good chance that you'll hire your artist back on, eventually because the pressure of trying to do both jobs on a game project will likely turn your brain into tapioca pudding.

2.2.3 Pixel Hobbyists

Whether you are looking to break into game development or simply a Pixel Art enthusiast, this book lays it all out for you. Even if you have been building with pixels actively for years, you are likely to find techniques within that will help you build faster and more efficiently.

2.2.4 Indie Developers

It is for you, more than anyone else that I have written this book.

As an indie developer, you are involved intimately with every aspect of your product. This book will help raise the quality and consistency of your aesthetic, reduce the file sizes of your art assets, and improve your bowling game. Except it won't improve your bowling game. I just got a little excited.

2.3 HOW TO USE THIS BOOK?

This book lays out foundational concepts in each chapter that build upon the last. Perhaps more significantly, the exercises become less and less focused on giving step-by-step instructions throughout the book. So by the end I'm hoping to cover more high level concepts without needing to show where to place each individual pixel or which buttons to press in the software.

To get the most out of your experience, I encourage readers to read straight through—completing each tutorial as they appear in sequence. I've broken Exercise 1 into four subsections, having each subsection follow the chapter explaining how to do the relevant set of tasks.

That being said, you bought the book and have the unique privilege to do whatever the heck you want with it—after all, you bought it. You may choose to skip around to sections relevant to what you are working on or ignore everything except the tutorials. You may choose to read it from back to front or use the pages of this book to create origami swans. I will say that it makes a great gift for your friends and family and highly encourage you to buy several copies.

CHAPTER 3

Who Am I and Why Do I Know So Much about Pixel Art?

Who am I? Where am I and what was I doing again? Come to think of it, how the hell did I get here? Where did I leave my keys? Brace yourself for the backstory. Maybe you want to get some chamomile tea or something to help settle you in for this heartwarming tale.

Many years ago I was an art student with the intention of becoming a painter. I studied all about how to use traditional renaissance techniques to create nifty artwork and avoided anything about how to apply what was learned practically (i.e., how to get a job). So focused were my passions that I convinced my academic adviser that it was in my best interest to postpone all of my prerequisite classes and take only art and music courses (for a while I was considering a music major before realizing that I had paralyzing stage fright). Among my courses was a 3D graphics course at the Art Academy of Cincinnati that indirectly altered my professional course for ever after.

After school I found that my myopic focus on art had left me at a slight (read major) disadvantage when entering the job market. The only skill that I could isolate as directly marketable was my new familiarity with 3D modeling. So I took classes and bought a computer to build work to improve my 3D portfolio.

At some juncture, due to my 3D work, I landed an interview at a game company in Virginia. Before that moment I had never realized that game development could be a profession and was enamored by the marriage of technology and creativity. Although I did not get the job, I had decided that this was going to be my profession. This seemed like something I could study my whole life without ever running out of new information or having it get stale. Although at that point I didn't really have enough experience to be very valuable in the game industry, so I resolved to go back to school.

Several years later I loaded my wife, dog, two cats, and 4-month-old daughter into a plane heading toward Vancouver, BC to study art and animation for game development at the Art Institute of Vancouver. It was an amazing adventure where I learned a lot more tricks and tools for creating 3D art and animation. At that point in time there really weren't many schools that taught game development. There were a few options, but each of them had some aspect that was not ideal for my situation. That particular Art Institute had a practicum where you actually build a video game as part of the curriculum—and that really sold it for me. I was older than most of my classmates and a couple of them called me "Old Man Silber," but it was an incredible experience that transformed me professionally.

I believe that now a lot of the game development classes have cross pollinated across the Art Institute schools (as well as other schools) and there are more options for studying game art and animation, so if you ever chose that path you may not need to move across the country. So I studied a great many aspects of game development, concentrating on 3D art because that *seemed* to be the ticket to getting hired in the game industry.

Then after school I landed my first job in game development at Handheld Games, where I worked as a Pixel Artist and did no 3D work at all. I loved it and fell in love with this idiosyncratic media. Over the next two years I worked on more than a half dozen commercial video games. While working at Handheld Games I'd been credited on Nintendo DS, Nintendo GBA, Vmigo, and "plug and play" games with licenses that include Marvel, Disney, Pixar, and Nicktoons.

During that time period I created Pixel Art animations and environments for 8(+) hours a day, 5(+) days a week and learned the idiosyncrasies of the medium while on the job. A few things were shared by my coworkers, but mostly I learned the hard way—with lots of trial and error.

Since then, I've founded the game company Interstellar Tortoise LLC and written some small "indie" games like Pixel Guy's Quest. I love the Pixel Art aesthetic and want to do what I can to assist the developer community in getting the most out of this magnificent style of graphics.

DISCLAIMER(S)

As with any creative discipline, there is a large subjective component. There are some techniques and explanations in which I expect some dissent—and that is perfectly fine. I've tried my best to give guidance and examples that will be useful, and don't feel that these are the only strong solutions. Take the principles that work for you and feel free to dump the rest.

I've also made some minor mistakes on some of the artwork in the pages of this book. At times I had to intentionally sacrifice some aspect of quality in order to spend the time to make clear the relevant example. The process of writing this book was a huge effort and sometimes I didn't have the time to use best practices while creating examples. Work with me and look for the point I'm trying to make.

CHAPTER 4

Software

Set Up Your Working Environment

YOU MAY BE WONDERING what to use to build your Pixel Art creations. Put away your graph paper because there are a gaggle of software packages that are available for free or for cheap specifically built around creating Pixel Art. All of these can be set up quickly and easily and each has positives and negatives.

The tools you choose to create with are up to you, so I've taken effort to make the teaching as ubiquitous as possible. In the fast-moving environment of the tech world, software changes but underlying principles outlined throughout the book should endure. That being said, I'll give my two cents on the software that will turn you into a lean, mean, pixel machine the fastest.

4.1 WHAT *NOT* TO USE

Brace yourself: I strongly encourage you *not* to use Photoshop or Gimp.

This suggestion may trigger an anaphylactic shock in some, but let me preface that I absolutely love these programs—but they are not easily set up to create Pixel Art. You are the one affected most by your choice, so what you choose is completely up to you—but some choices will lead you down a road to heartache, leaving you unemployed in Greenland.

Do not use any program built for creating Vector Art. This would include Illustrator, Incscape, or virtually any piece of software with the work "vector" in the name.

4.2 MY SOFTWARE RECOMMENDATION

My strong suggestion for most of you is a program called GraphicsGale.

This program is very well rounded for creating Pixel Art and the free version has everything you need to start rocking out with Pixel Art.

Navigate to the following webpage and download GraphicsGale: http://www.humanbalance.net/gale/us/download.html

Note: Be sure to click the "Get Free" button rather than the "Try Shareware" so that you will avoid needing to make changes later.

4.3 OTHER OPTIONS FOR PIXEL ART SOFTWARE

Although GraphicsGale if fabulous, there are many other options depending on your needs and preferences.

If you know you are going to be spending a lot of time on Pixel Art, you should consider spending the $100 (at the time of this printing) to buy Pro Motion (currently my favorite and what I use most of the time). Pyxel Edit is an excellent tool specifically for creating environmental tile maps where you can lay out your entire scene and any changes made to one tile will automatically update all of that time of file within the scene. Piq is a tool available and usable online—where you won't need to install any software on your computer—if that is something that appeals to you. There are also mobile phone options for Pixel editing on the go, such as Pixel Art editor, Pixel Create, or Pixelesque.

There are also many others, including Grafx2, Asprite, Paint.NET, and too many others to list them all. Many of them have both good qualities and drawbacks so feel free to try a few and you may be surprised that certain techniques are easier or more difficult to do in various programs.

At the time of writing this, GraphicsGale does not run on Mac, so those of you eating Apples will have to investigate one of these other options—there is a long list of Pixel Art programs discussed in Chapter 12.

4.4 A BRIEF GLANCE AT GRAPHICSGALE

Although this is not intended to be a book about software, I wanted to point out some of the tools used most commonly throughout our Pixel Art journey—and where to find them within the GraphicsGale program.

In Figure 4.1, I've labeled some of the more important tools you'll need in GraphicsGale. I am pretty confident that even if you aren't using this software you'll find something similar in the program you're using. That's what I like about you—you're resourceful.

FIGURE 4.1   The GraphicsGale main interface.

A. Drawing tool

B. Straight line tool

C. Fill tool

D. Rectangular marquee

E. Show grid

F. File save

G. File open

H. New file

And one last important note—In GraphicsGale you should get familiar with the magical "assign hotkey" tool shown in Figure 4.2, accessible in the "Preferences" menu (Figure 4.3). You can even assign a hotkey to make this menu pop up (you can see that I've chosen the character A for that purpose).

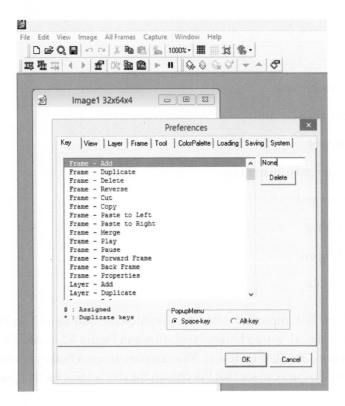

FIGURE 4.2   Set hotkeys for commonly used actions.

FIGURE 4.3   GraphicsGale sets hotkeys in the "Preferences" menu.

Even if the program you are using does not allow you to set your hotkeys, it is well worth the time to learn the default hotkeys and integrate them into your workflow. Don't complain, just do it. You'll thank me later. You'll probably even offer to buy me a drink if you see me (which is not so unlikely as you'd think as the game dev community is surprisingly small).

CHAPTER 5

Making Pixel Art

Doing Lines

PUT AWAY THE MIRROR and razor, that stuff will kill your brain. There are a few idiosyncrasies of drawing with pixels that are easy to conquer if you know what to expect. Curves and diagonal lines can be a bit challenging to create when the available resource is nothing but squares.

I will now share one super helpful command in GraphicsGale that will become a huge convenience. When using the pen tool, the right mouse button can be used as an eyedropper tool. That is to say that when the right mouse button is pressed, it will pick up whatever color was underneath it and make that currently selected color. Over time you will see that this is super swanky.

5.1 STRAIGHT LINES

You may not be able to draw a straight line on paper, but straight lines are easy with Pixel Art! Click the "Connect Line" button in your tool window or press the appropriate hotkey to go to the straight line tool. Not too hard to begin with, but you can also press the "Shift" button to have the lines snap into vertical or horizontal position (Figure 5.1).

FIGURE 5.1   Use the SHIFT key to lock lines horizontally or vertically.

5.2 DIAGONAL LINES

Diagonal lines take a bit more attention but there are some best practices that can be followed.

Use equal segment lengths whenever possible (Figures 5.2 and 5.3):

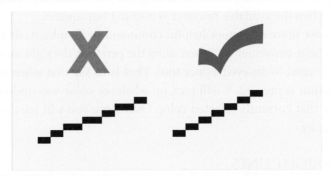

FIGURE 5.2   Consistent step pattern gives better line quality.

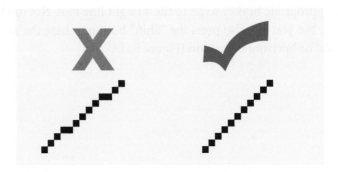

FIGURE 5.3   Avoid using inconsistent step patterns.

When equal space is not possible, alternate between two segment lengths, and this will be the case from time to time because you may need to create an angle that isn't adequately described with equal line lengths (Figure 5.4).

FIGURE 5.4   Sometimes you may need to alternate step lengths.

5.3 CURVED LINES

I'm not going to lie—curved lines are a major pain in the butt. Creating the feel of a curve using nothing but right angles borders on lunacy—but we can still make them look adequate if we follow some guidelines.

5.3.1 Avoid the Lone Wolf

When one pixel sticks out, it's going to undermine the illusion of curve, and look ugly. Avoid the lone pixel (Figure 5.5).

FIGURE 5.5   Avoid the lone pixel.

5.3.2 Make Each Segment Length Progressively Longer or Shorter

This really assists the curviness of the line. Sometimes it won't be possible with a given shape, but it is something to strive for (Figures 5.6 and 5.7).

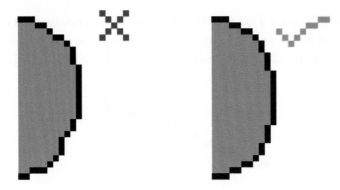

FIGURE 5.6   Curves are difficult.

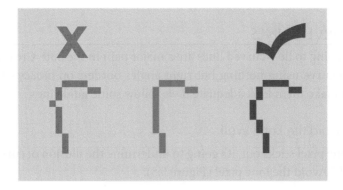

FIGURE 5.7   Small adjustments affect line quality.

5.3.3 Beware the Circle Tool

Many programs have some kind of curve tool and/or circle tool, and I recommend that you use it with trepidation. Although it can be helpful, in most cases you will want to go back and adjust the lines so they follow the guidelines we've been talking about. In Figure 5.8 you can observe that though circular, the circle tool does not necessarily have fabulous line quality.

FIGURE 5.8   The circle tool in most programs have mediocre line quality.

5.3.4 Make Love with the Cut and Paste Features

(That's intended figuratively, by the way.) Converse to the circle tool, cutting and pasting your work (often after rotating or mirroring it) will always be up to your exacting standards and will get maximum bang for your buck. Cutting and pasting work also allows you to expend effort once and get the benefits repeatedly.

5.4 LINE WIDTH

If you hadn't noticed from the screenshots shown so far, each line is only 1 pixel wide. This is usually the more desirable aesthetic for a line. In this case, having a thicker girth does not work in your favor, no matter what the ladies or lads say (Figure 5.9).

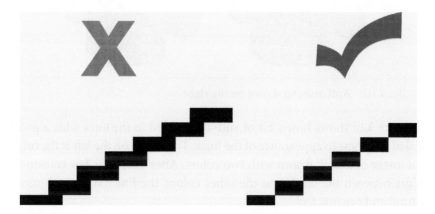

FIGURE 5.9   One pixel line width is usually desirable.

This idea of having a one pixel line width is not a hard rule so much as a guideline that seems to be preferable in most circumstances. It's really more of a flaccid rule.

5.5 ANTI-ALIASING

Anti-alias is the expression used for when extra pixels are used to soften the angular edges of a line, the result being a sharper looking edge. In many software packages this process is done automatically by a filter within the program (this is why text looks so sharp in word processing programs).

The process is actually quite simple. Create a color that is a blend between the line color and the background color and use that color to soften some or all of the steps of a line.

To give additional sharpness to the line you may choose to use a second color to blend between the midtone and the background and use it for more than one pixel length.

Just be careful not to overuse anti-alias, because too much will cause your picture to look blurry. A little bit can go a long way and it is fairly easy to go overboard. One thing that can help tremendously is to zoom out from the picture occasionally to see how the image looks from far away.

FIGURE 5.10   Anti-aliasing shown on the right.

Figure 5.10 shows how a bit of anti-alias added to the lines adds a good deal of crispness to appearance of the lines. The image on the left is the original image of a skull drawn with two colors. After adding as few transition colors between the black and the other colors, the line has a much more natural and organic feel.

So, when working with lines there are a number of guidelines that help to give desirable results. Avoid the lone wolf pixel, beware the circle tool, be mindful of pixel width, and get comfy with the cut and paste features and you'll do just fine. Use anti-alias when needed (but don't overdo it) and try to gradually use longer lines when you're making curves.

EXERCISE 5.1: CREATING A LINE DRAWING SPRITE

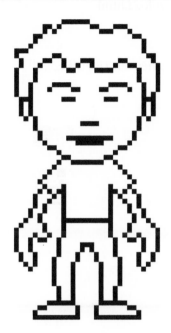

FIGURE E5.1 The line drawing we'll build in this chapter.

FIGURE E5.2 In later chapters we'll add light, shadow, and color.

We have to get started building something, so we're going to create a character. More specifically, we are going to build the character shown in Figure E5.1. Later we'll add some color to this dude so he looks more polished, so that he'll end up looking like Figure E5.2, but that will be over the course of a few exercises. For the time being, we're going to focus on building this sprite with line.

You may be concerned if you are new to the art side of development, but don't get bent out of shape because we are going to build it in stages. For now we are going to focus only on drawing the outline of the sprite, applying the line techniques we've talked about up until this point.

Step 0: Download and Install GraphicsGale or Other Pixel Art Software

We covered this earlier, so if you are reading this book cover to cover, you should already be ready for business. But in case you missed it, navigate to the following webpage and download the software:
http://www.humanbalance.net/gale/us/download.html

Step 1: Create a New Project

Go to **File—New...** or hit Ctrl+N to create a new file (Figure E5.3).

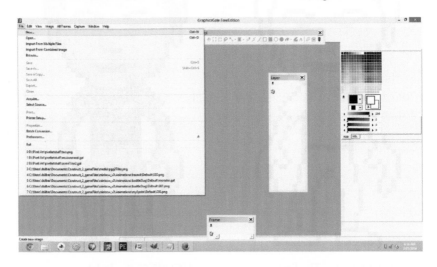

FIGURE E5.3   Create a new file.

A dialogue window will pop up with some options. We want the dimensions to be 32 pixels wide and 64 pixels high with 4-bit color as shown in Figure E5.4.

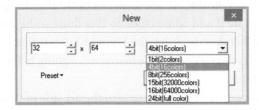

FIGURE E5.4   Use 4-bit color for this sprite.

Choosing 4-bit color will give us a palette of only eight colors, which will help to keep the file size small and our options limited so that we won't get overwhelmed. You should now see a vertically oriented canvas similar to what you see in Figure E5.5.

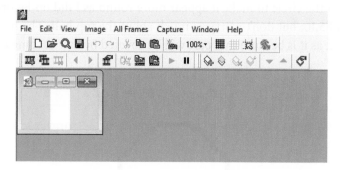

FIGURE E5.5

Use the magnifying glass icon (or map hotkeys in the preferences menu) to zoom in or out of the canvas so that the white rectangle takes up the majority of the screen like in Figure E5.6.

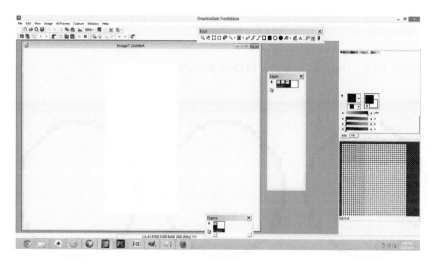

FIGURE E5.6   Zoom in so you can see what you're doing.

Step 2: Draw a Head and Face

A quick bit of advice, before we get too far: don't worry about the speed of completion while trying to learn technique. Speed comes from a solid mental concept of what to do, and that only comes with time. Since we're just covering the core concepts you may as well slow down and enjoy the ride!

Use the circle tool to draw a large circle on the canvas similar to Figure E5.7, which will be our character's head. You may need to adjust the bottom of the circle to make it appear more round as I did on Figures E5.8 through E5.10, but don't worry as much about the top half. The head area can be left as it is because that part will be covered by hair at some point.

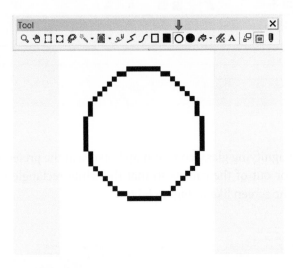

FIGURE E5.7   Use the circle tool to draw a circle.

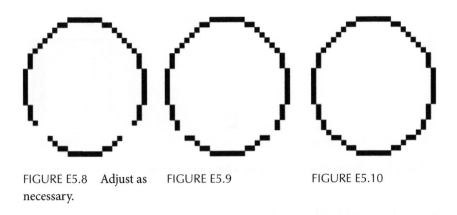

FIGURE E5.8   Adjust as   FIGURE E5.9   FIGURE E5.10
necessary.

The eyes should be about half way between the top and bottom of the circle (Figure E5.11) and can be represented with just a couple pixels for each eye like in Figure E5.12.

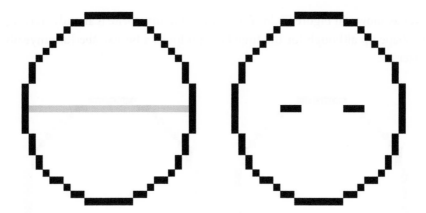

FIGURE E5.11   Eyes will be halfway up the head.

FIGURE E5.12   Eyes without a face.

Keep in mind that we are drawing this character looking straight ahead. If we were to draw the character looking up or down, the line of where we'd see the eyes in the context of the rest of the face would change as shown in Figure E5.13. You can see how if the character looks up, the eye line is raised and when the character looks down, the eyes are lower within the circle of the head.

FIGURE E5.13   The eye position changes if the character looks up or down.

As you can see in Figure E5.14 about half way between the eyes and the bottom of the chin is the nose. About half way between the nose and the chin is the mouth, as shown in Figure E5.15. Keep in mind that these are simply guidelines and could change depending on the character or if the head were in a different position. Next we'll add eyebrows just a couple pixels above the eyes as shown in Figure E5.16. You can see that this sprite is already starting to shape up although for the time being it looks a bit like the RummyKub joker tile.

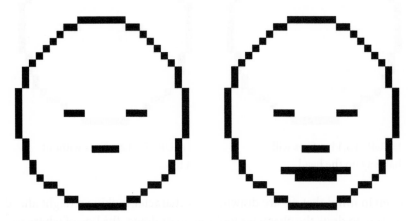

FIGURE E5.14   The bottom of the nose is about halfway between the head and chin.

FIGURE E5.15   The mouth is about halfway between the bottom of the nose and chin.

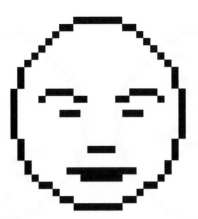

FIGURE E5.16   Add eyebrows.

Rather than adding the hair and tightening the face, I want to get the whole character roughed out. After drawing the rest of the body we may decide that the head is too big or too small or simply doesn't fit—so it is useful not to spend too much time on detail until we lay out the entire character.

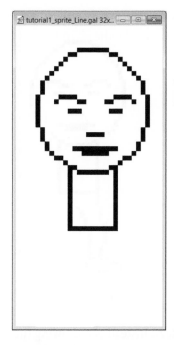

FIGURE E5.17   His torso is a rectangle.

Step 3: Draw the Body

We'll start by drawing the torso simply as a square as in Figure E5.17. Later we can do some rearranging if we choose, but most likely we won't need to. Working with pixels should be simple. Sometimes I mess up that part and make things too complicated, but in general it is better to KISS—keep it simple, stupid!

Next we'll draw one leg and foot as shown in Figures E5.18 through E5.20. Again notice that we really don't have to do anything elaborate. That is one of the sterling qualities of working with Pixel Art: we can really do a lot with a simple drawing. Later, we'll add some detail in the form of texture and shadow but I'll iterate that it is super useful to keep things straightforward.

FIGURE E5.18   FIGURE E5.19   FIGURE E5.20

Now we can start our journey toward being lazy. Instead of redrawing the leg, we are going to duplicate the leg and then flip it to save us the effort of doing this a second time.

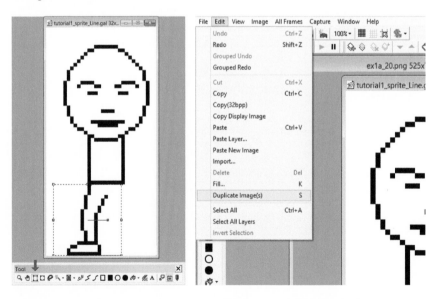

FIGURE E5.21   Use the marquee   FIGURE E5.22   Duplicate the leg.
tool to select the leg.

You're still new so I'll walk you through this process in GraphicsGale. First we're going to use the rectangular selection tool to select the leg as shown in Figure E5.21. Next use the **Edit** dropdown menu and choose **Duplicate Image(s)** as shown in Figure E5.22. It will likely put the new section right on top of the old one so you may not see that it's been duplicated until it has been moved. Drag the extra leg to roughly the correct position as in Figure E5.23 and go to the **Image** dropdown menu to select **Flip Horizontal** as shown in Figure E5.24. This should yield a result somewhat like Figure E5.25.

FIGURE E5.23   FIGURE E5.24   Flip the leg horizontally.

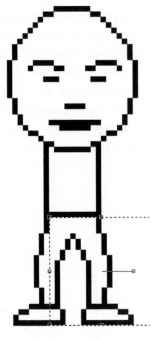

FIGURE E5.25   Place the leg.

FIGURE E5.26   Adjust as needed.

This doesn't save us a ton effort in this example but for a more complicated image it would, and it will be good to get comfortable with this process. As a game artist, you should always be on the lookout for tools and techniques that will get the job done quicker. The less time you spend on any individual aspect, the more time you have to allocate toward polish or overall quality.

You'll see I've also done a slight adjustment to the crotch in Figure E5.26 to complete the image—but you can make your own judgment as to whether your crotch needs adjustment.

Now we are going to repeat the process with the arms and hands. First, we'll draw the outline of an arm (Figure E5.27) and then we'll adjust the pixels so that the arm appears to connect to the body by deleting the vertical line as shown in Figure E5.28. And with only a few more pixels, we'll give the impression of hand as shown in Figure E5.29.

FIGURE E5.27   FIGURE E5.28   FIGURE E5.29

In screenshots in Figures E5.30 through E5.32, we're creating a sleeve for the character. I've added a few pixels as needed, then erased out the ones we don't want in order to give an edge to the character's sleeve.

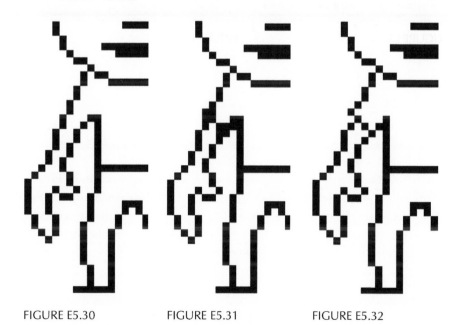

FIGURE E5.30   FIGURE E5.31   FIGURE E5.32

Now that we have an arm that looks pretty good, we're going to select it (Figure E5.33), duplicate it, paste it, flip it horizontal, and place it on the other side (Figures E5.33 and E5.34). This should seem familiar, as it is almost identical to how we handled the leg earlier in this exercise. If this seems new, then I fear you may have fallen asleep for a couple minutes back there.

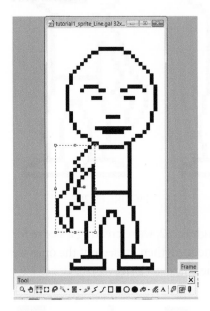

FIGURE E5.33

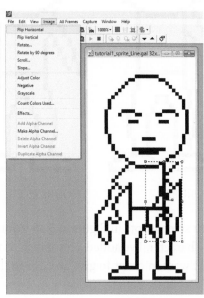

FIGURE E5.34

FIGURE E5.35

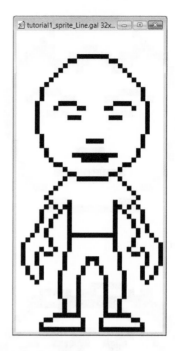

FIGURE E5.36

The last thing that we need to do is to erase the extra line(s) from the shoulder as shown in Figure E5.36. Shazam! We've got the character's line drawing almost totally complete!

Hmmm... But we should probably give this character some hair. We're going to deal with this hair in a very particular way—by drawing the inside line of where the hair overlaps the forehead, then the outside outline of the hair creating the sides and top of the head. It may seem a bit unintuitive, but stay with me—I've got a plan.

We'll start by outlining where the hair will fall on the forehead. We don't have to be too anal retentive, just rough it out like in Figure E5.37. In Figure E5.38, I've drawn out the general shape of the top of the hair and put in nubbins that will become ears. Notice that the bottom of the ears are more or less at the same level as the nose. The top of the ears are often close to the same level as the eyes or eyebrows. You'll notice in Figure E5.39 how messy the initial drawing can be, but that is okay. Just use the guidelines discussed in the early chapter on lines to clean up the line work, as shown in Figure E5.40.

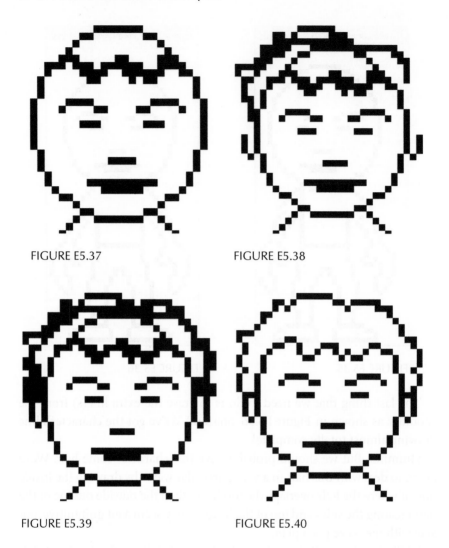

FIGURE E5.37

FIGURE E5.38

FIGURE E5.39

FIGURE E5.40

And violà—faster than a speeding turtle, we're done with the line drawing of our sprite!

CHAPTER 6

Coloring inside the Lines

B Y THIS TIME YOU may be getting sick of working only with lines (I know I am!), so let's get started with some color and tone. As with most aspects of Pixel Art, we can learn to do a lot with a little, and color choice is no exception.

Let's get started with a new file to get comfortable with our palette options before adding color to our character.

Go to **File—New** or hit Ctrl+N to create a new file (Figure 6.1).

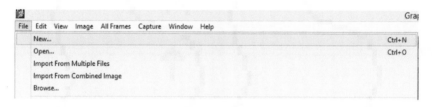

FIGURE 6.1   Ctrl + N to create a new file.

6.1 4-BIT PALETTE

A dialogue window will pop up with some options. For now I'm going to make the dimensions to be 32 pixels wide and 32 pixels high, but it doesn't really matter what size the canvas is for this particular chapter.

But before hitting the "OK" button, let's take a look at the last drop-down option. It may be hard to notice in Figure 6.2 due to the available options, but each bit doubles the number of colors. 1 bit is 2 colors, 2 bits would be 4 colors, 3 bits would be 8 colors, 4 bits is 16 colors, etc.

FIGURE 6.2   4 bits = 16 colors.

We're going to work in 4 bits (16 colors) for now to make things as clear as possible.

6.2 FILL TOOL

Start by drawing some sort of closed shape like the left image in Figure 6.3. We will avoid open shapes like the picture on the right so that the "fill tool" (also called the "paint bucket tool" in some programs) will color in the object without coloring the entire background.

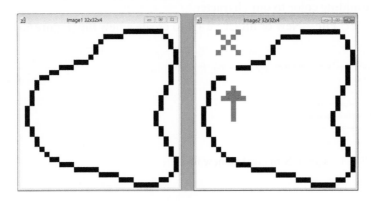

FIGURE 6.3   A closed shape is shown on the left.

The fill tool (or "flood fill" or "paint bucket") allows us to add color to an entire area rather than trying to fill in the space one pixel at a time. Figure 6.4 shows what the tool icon looks like in GraphicsGale, but it may appear different depending on which Pixel Art software you are using. Figure 6.5 shows the final result after using the tool.

Cosmigo Pro Motion (another Pixel Art program discussed earlier in this book) has additional fill tool options like filling only the outline or filling in a gradient in addition to filling a single color. The outline fill has become of my most commonly used tools.

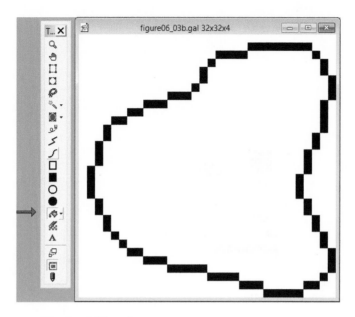

FIGURE 6.4   The flood fill tool.

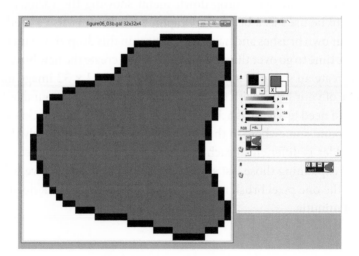

FIGURE 6.5   A flood filled shape.

Figure 6.6 gives us a detail of the palette area, which has some pretty important stuff for pixel artists. On the top row is the list of available colors. There are only 16 colors available to us because we are using a 4-bit palette. If we were using an 8-bit palette, there would be 256 colors shown in this area.

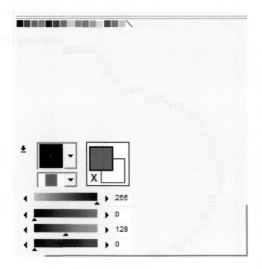

FIGURE 6.6   A 4-bit palette.

In Figure 6.7, we see a drop-down menu showing the various shapes available to be used as a brush. In GraphicsGale there is also a method to create your own brushes and have them appear in this drop-down menu. We don't have time to go over the steps in detail but to create the new brush you'd have to create an shape as a 1-bit (black and white) 32 × 32 image making the shape of your brush with the white pixels and the background as black. Then you'd need to save it as a .bmp file and drop it into GraphicGale's "pen" folder—found somewhere in the "AppData" folder. Unfortunately the path to that folder is different in each operating system but you can easily find a tutorial explaining those last steps online. For the most part we will only be using the one pixel brush anyway, so I'm not going to track down these pieces of minutia.

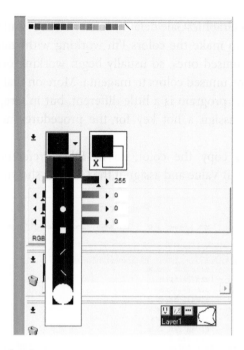

FIGURE 6.7   Brush selection.

Next to the drop-down menu there is a black square overlapping a white square with an X in the lower left corner; this is showing the current colors being used. The color on the top square is the color currently selected to draw with. The color in the background is a second color that can be used for creating patterns and if you click on the image of the X the two colors will swap positions, which can be useful in some circumstances.

6.3 CREATING GRADIENTS

A gradient is a smooth transition between two colors. But with Pixel Art we have a limited number of colors to work with, so the transition seldom tends to be particularly smooth. The term "ramp" is commonly used in place of "gradient" to describe the set of colors that blend together from one color to the next like in Figure 6.8.

FIGURE 6.8   A color gradient or "ramp."

The palette in GraphicsGale defaults to something similar to Figure 6.5. I find it helpful to make the colors I'm working with stand out dramatically from the unused ones, so usually begin working on my palette by changing all of the unused colors to magenta. More on that later.

Every Pixel Art program is a little different, but in GraphicsGale, we'll want to quickly assign a hot key for the procedures needed to create gradients:

We'll need to copy the color, so in File—Preferences menu find Palette—Copy RGB Value and assign it the C key as shown in Figure 6.9.

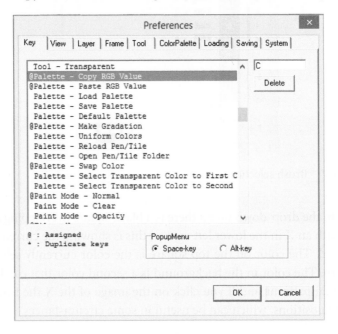

FIGURE 6.9   Setting a hotkey to Copy RGB Value.

- Next, assign the V key to the Palette—Paste RGB Value on the line below as shown in Figure 6.10.

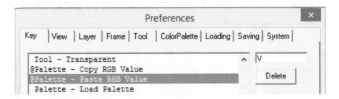

FIGURE 6.10   Setting a hotkey to Paste RGB Value.

- And finally we'll assign the R key to the Palette—Make Gradation Line as shown in Figure 6.11.

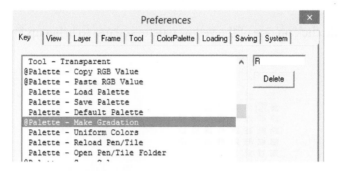

FIGURE 6.11   Setting a hotkey to Make Gradation.

Frequently you'll want to copy a color to a new location on the palette and lighten or darken it to make the two ends of the gradient. Because this is such a common practice, we'll run through once as a very quick example of how to use these hot keys.

Left click on the yellow color in the palette window to select it.

Press the "C" key on the keyboard to copy the color.

Left click on the light grey color and press "V" to paste the yellow color into that palette position.

Figure 6.12 window will pop up to confirm your selection. Make sure "Paste to first color" is selected, and hit okay.

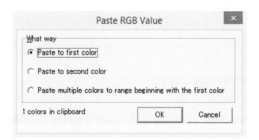

FIGURE 6.12   Pasting the color to a new palette location.

Now your palette should have two yellows in it, like in Figure 6.13.

FIGURE 6.13   The yellow color has been duplicated.

Double click on one of the yellow palette squares to bring up Figure 6.14.

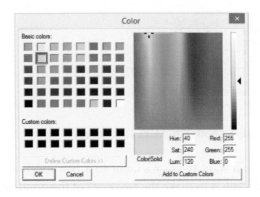

FIGURE 6.14   Making one of the colors darker.

Drag the slider on the right down to make the yellow a darker shade and hit OK.

Now to create a ramp between the two shades of yellow, left click on the one of the yellows, then right click on the other yellow and click the "R" key. The window shown in Figure 6.15 should pop up to confirm the action.

FIGURE 6.15   Confirm your action.

If everything worked as it should, your palette should now look like Figure 6.16.

FIGURE 6.16   A gradient has been created.

We now have five shades of yellow that we can use to create texture or shade in lemons, sunflowers, bananas, urine, etc. Really you can use this to create anything golden that showers your mind!

FIGURE 6.17   Lemon built from a five color ramp.

6.4 PALETTE SWAPPING

At this point I will be using the terms ramp and gradient interchange-ably, so be on your toes. Ramps are super useful when creating Pixel Art. Gradients can be used on individual sprites to show texture and lighting as shown on the lemon in Figure 6.17 but their real utility comes in the form of organization and ease of iteration.

It is actually extremely important to keep your colors organized, and allow me to explain why. Let's say we have a simple background as shown in Figure 6.18.

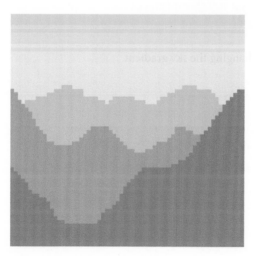

FIGURE 6.18   A simple background.

It's a nice background but now we decide that we really want the sky to be a sunset. If we have a neatly organized palette like this one does, then we are set up to make changes speedy quick! The palette for this image is shown in Figure 6.19. The four colors on the left were created with a ramp for the mountain colors, and the four-color gradient on the right make the sky colors.

FIGURE 6.19   The four left colors make the sky.

To create our sunset, all you would need to do is to change the two end colors of the sky gradient to the desirable colors like in Figure 6.20 and ramp them together so they look like in Figure 6.21.

FIGURE 6.20   Change the end colors of the sky gradient.

FIGURE 6.21   Changing the sky gradient.

And viola, we've got a sunset in just a few moments as seen in Figure 6.22!

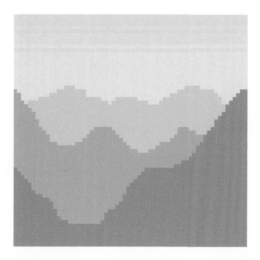

FIGURE 6.22   Change the colors, change your scene.

To further illustrate the point, let's say we want to keep both the first background and the sunset version of the image... And the producer wants you to create a nighttime version of the environment as well. This is no problem for you, the image is already built! You make some variations to the palette so now it looks like Figure 6.23.

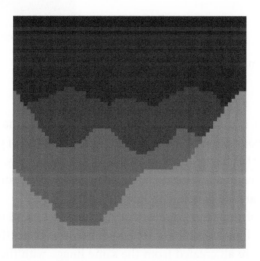

FIGURE 6.23   Easy background change.

You simply use the three palettes to change the same picture to suit your needs as shown in Figure 6.24.

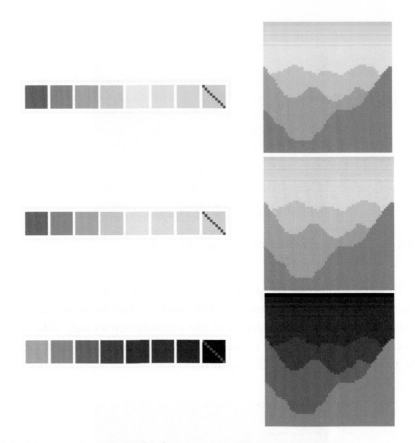

FIGURE 6.24   An organized palette improves life.

This concept is called "palette swapping" and can dramatically expand the content in your game. We've seen that for the creation of game environments, it is easy to change the appearance of the time of day. This gives the possibility of having a level of your game reused within your game while giving the appearance of being unique art assets.

The beauty of this technique is that it works just as easily for complicated scenes, so long as you have set up your palette correctly. Figures 6.25 through 6.27 were all created from the same image with the palette being swapped to create the dramatic differences in the scenery.

FIGURE 6.25   City scene.

FIGURE 6.26   City scene with palette adjustment.

FIGURE 6.27   City scene with another palette adjustment.

This same technique can be used for characters or enemies in your game. Your programmer can code some unique behaviors, but the sprite can be reused with a simple palette swap. This means that you can potentially circumvent the process of designing and creating all animations for several entire characters in your game.

If you are sneaky, you can entirely change a sprite by simply changing the palette. In Figure 6.28, you can see four characters—but in truth it was literally built with only one image using a palette that changes drastically to create each variation.

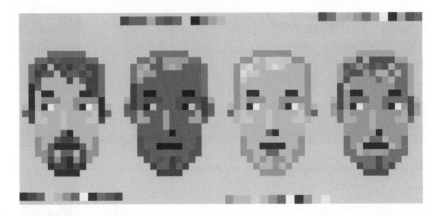

FIGURE 6.28   Same head, different palettes.

The key to obtaining this kind of dramatic result is to have colors that are different on one palette—such as the beard and the skin tone—be a duplicate of the same color on the next palette. Figure 6.29 shows the exact same effect but simplified for clarity. In this figure, we start with the bearded character on the left, using a three-color palette. In the center image we've changed the beard color to the same color as the skin tone—and I've outlined the shape to show which pixels would change appearance. And to the right we see the final result of the effort. There are still three colors in the palette, but two of them will be identical so that they can be swapped to create the bearded version.

FIGURE 6.29   Sneaky palette tricks.

6.5 PALETTE SIZE AND TIME CONSIDERATION

When it comes to creating a palette, the first thing you should be asking yourself is how few colors you can get away with for the image. Keeping your palette as small as possible strongly works in your favor in terms of speed and ease of production. The more colors you use, the more there is to keep track of and the harder it is to remain consistent. This becomes particularly difficult when attempting to keep colors consistent while animating.

Of course, the more complex an image is, the more colors you'll need to give the desired effect.

Take a look at Figure 6.30. This character's head is built 32 × 32 pixel large in all three panels, but you can see there is a great volatility in the amount of detail. The first image uses only 3 colors to make the head, the second image uses 5 colors, and the third image uses 11. As you can see, more colors allows a higher degree of visual complexity.

FIGURE 6.30   More colors = more complexity.

It seems nice—and the results can be lovely—but the extra colors come at a price. Each of these images took exponentially longer to create as the last. The first image took me about 5 minutes to build, the second image took about 10 minutes, and the third about a half hour. Consider the additional time it would take to create the rest of the character (roughly double the time). If you were to create an eight-frame walking animation, that would end up being:

- (5 minutes for the head + 10 minutes for the body) × 8 frames = 120 minutes or 2 hours
- (10 minutes for the head + 20 minutes for the body) × 8 frames = 240 minutes or 4 hours
- (30 minutes for the head + 60 minutes for the body) × 8 frames = 720 minutes or 12 hours

Now if we consider that this character would likely need multiple animations such as a jump, an idle, an attack, an animation for taking damage, etc.—you can see that the amount of time it takes to draw each frame becomes a major consideration.

I'll be honest—as much as I like the highly detailed version of the head, I would not want to animate that dude (at least not on a tight schedule).

One thing to note is that all of the characters and environments within a game should have a consistent style. Now think reflect on all of the sprites in your entire game and consider the difference in time to create them at different levels of detail. It is worth your while to determine the size of your palette early in your project before you become committed to creating an onslaught of overly complicated character animations.

That extra time consideration at the onset of your project can quite literally be the difference in completing or not completing your game. What's more, you can make one decision that saves you a lot of time and effort in the months or years to come.

6.6 CHOOSING COLORS

The most common way of creating a palette that I see in Pixel Art is also the most straightforward: to create a gradient from dark to light for each object color used. Figure 6.31 gives a very simple example of this idea and we'll take a moment to talk about that palette.

FIGURE 6.31   Sprite built using color ramps.

The palette for this sprite consists of four gradients and one extra color. In this example, each gradient is used to describe exactly one sort of item. The three blues are used to create the pants, the oranges for the hair, and the four beige colors for the skin tones. One thing I've found is skin tones benefit from being a tighter gradient (meaning less change from one color to the next) and having more colors. This seems to be true regardless of the actual skin type you are trying to create. The only reuse of color is the purple used for the shoes and the eyes.

If we take a look at Figure 6.32, we see that the palette was built in the same manor—with each ramp describing one thing, using different gradients for the grass as the tree foliage. Every color gradient was built from dark to light but that is not the only way to create a gradient. In Figure 6.33, we have taken the blue colors that are used in the sky and ramped them from blue to pink instead of dark to light; and the result is quite lovely. This would be described as a ramp that makes a change in *hue* rather than a change in *value*.

FIGURE 6.32   Sky ramps value.   FIGURE 6.33   Sky ramps hue.

Let's just take a moment to talk about hue and value...and saturation as well. If we double click on one of the colors in the palette window, then we get a window like in Figure 6.34 that allows us to manipulate the color in more detail.

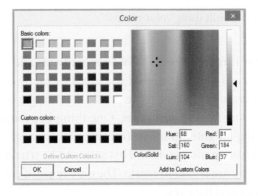

FIGURE 6.34

That large box with rainbow-esque colors has arranged the colors in a particular way, which helps to get the colors you're looking for once you become accustomed to it.

Figure 6.35 explains that as we move left to right the colors change hue, and as we move up and down the colors change saturation.

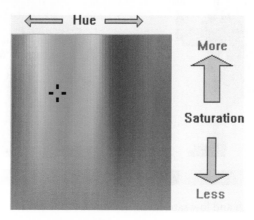

FIGURE 6.35

You can see how all the colors get more intense as they get higher up on the chart—for this reason, saturation is sometimes called intensity. Also notice that the colors get more grey as they get to the bottom until they get entirely desaturated and hit a neutral grey.

This chart allows us to pick exactly the hue and saturation level (or intensity) of the color we want, but does not give any difference in value—and that is why there is a slider bar on the right side of the screen in Figure 6.35 also shown here.

Figure 6.36 shows a character sprite with two color palettes of different saturation levels. The palette on the left is very high intensity or high saturation. The character on the right is low saturation or low intensity. There will be times where you'll want colors to be high intensity and also situations where you want them to be low saturation, but frequently you'll want something in the middle for many of your colors. Neither the high saturation nor the low saturation look as appealing as the first appearance of this sprite in Figure 6.31.

FIGURE 6.36 High and low saturation.

There may be times where you want something to intentionally stand out, which could be done by having everything besides that part very low in saturation but having that one item be very high intensity.

As an example, we may want this character's hair to stand out boldly as a bright fiery orange. In this case, we could use a very saturated orange for the hair and mute the intensity of all the other colors like Figure 6.37. Figuring out the right balance for the context you are working in is the key.

FIGURE 6.37 Using saturation to make the hair stand out.

FIGURE 6.38

By now you should be getting a good feel for saturation, so let us now move on to talk a bit about value and contrast.

The slider on the right side of the screen (Figure 6.38) allows you to alter the value of any color you select. As you can see from the colors available on the slider, the term value refers to how light or dark a color is.

The amount of change from dark to light within your image is called **contrast**. The amount of contrast between the values within your picture will determine how much the image will "pop" and in which places that will occur. Figure 6.39 shows our sprite built with very low contrast on the left, good contrast in the middle, and very high contrast on the right.

The palette on the left with low contrast is not ideal, as the colors seem a bit homogonous. There isn't very much "pop" to the picture, and it probably could have been built adequately to this quality with less colors. The high contrast palette on the right has too much "pop" in too many places and looks a bit harsh. It may be possible to use this level of contrast if there were more colors to blend the lights and the darks, but as it stands it is sub-optimal to say the least. The value changes to the colors to do not read smoothly and the viewer will struggle to figure out where the important parts of the image are.

The middle palette is a much stronger solution for this sprite. The values of the color gradients naturally blend into each other and the light part of one gradient makes some contrast with the dark of another ramp.

FIGURE 6.39   Low, medium, and high contrast.

6.7 TRANSPARENCY

It is common to reserve the first color in your palette to be transparent; I usually leave this color magenta, but it could really be any color you choose. This is a necessity for sprites, as the actual shape of a sprite is always rectangular and the space around the object is transparent.

As an example, imagine if you are running your game with a static background and a character sprite on it similar to Figure 6.40. In constructing this scene, the sprite itself will be rectangular but not displaying the magenta pixels—as shown in Figure 6.41.

FIGURE 6.40   What the player sees.

FIGURE 6.41   How the scene is built.

The computer actually organizes the various objects on screen as layers and runs some images at a higher "level priority." This means that those images will appear in front of the other objects on screen. You can use Figure 6.42 to help conceptualize how the computer thinks about the sprite in relationship to the background.

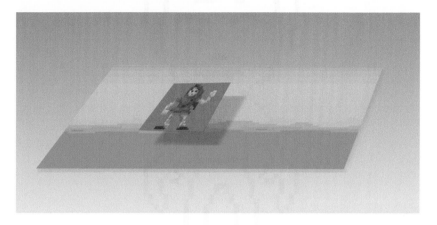

FIGURE 6.42   Games use layer priority to draw items on screen.

In this chapter we covered a lot of information about using color palettes in your Pixel Art. We talked about the difference between a 4-bit and 8-bit palette, how to use the fill tool, and the utility of working with gradients. We spent some talking about the amount of colors to use in your palette and how it's not the size but what you do with it that counts. We covered saturation and contrast and how to avoid choosing colors that look crappy for your artwork.

That chapter ended up being more saturated than I expected. My expectation was in full contrast with the reality and I didn't realize there was so much to cover about color.

EXERCISE 6.1: COLORING THE SPRITE (FROM EXERCISE 5.1)

FIGURE E6.1   Sprite from the Chapter 5 exercise.

Let's take a moment to admire our finished line drawing in (Figure E6.1). Ooh, ah... okay that's it, time to move along. It's time to fill this little dude in with color to give a bit more substance. This part of the exercise should be very short and to the point. Please feel free to write me a strongly worded email if I go too far into a tangential idea.

Now that we're working with color, there's one tool we're going to need to get cozy with: the flood fill tool. Sometimes it is called the paint bucket tool or simply the fill tool. Whatever it's called, this tool is the key to filling large volumes quickly. In GraphicsGale the button to use the tool looks like Figure E6.2.

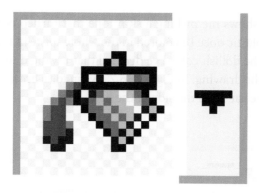

FIGURE E6.2   Our beloved "flood fill" tool.

Although this book concentrates on GraphicsGale, I do want to draw attention to another program called Pro Motion made by Cosmigo that has some really great fill tool features. In particular, there is an "Outline" mode that draws an outline around any pool of color which I've found to be particularly helpful. In this tutorial we've started with a line drawing and filled in the color, but frequently I'll start with blobs of color and use Pro Motion's special fill mode to create the outline afterward.

Next we'll pick colors for the character's shirt, pants, hair, and skin tone. As you should recall from the last chapter, you need only to double click on a color from your palette to bring up the color picker popup box.

I've used a very saturated but dark red for the pants (Figure E6.3) and a very grayish blue for the jeans (Figure E6.4).

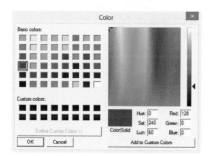 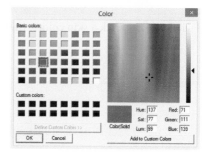

FIGURE E6.3   Choose a shirt color.   FIGURE E6.4   Choose a color for the pants.

Figure E6.5 shows me picking a skin tone that turned out to look a bit too much like plastic once I'd colored in the whole sprite in Figure E6.6. But in addition to the dollish color I've decided that I wanted to make a minor adjustment to the drawing. In Figure E6.7, I've made a break in the line that was dividing the ear from the side of the head.

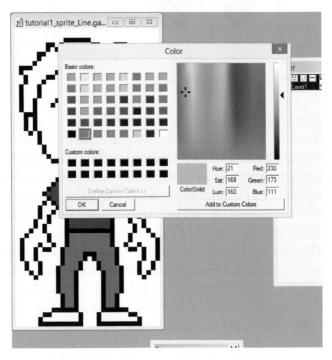

FIGURE E6.5   Pick a skin color—they're all pretty good.

FIGURE E6.6   Fill in the
sprite.

FIGURE E6.7   Adjust the
ears.

FIGURE E6.8   Organized gradients.

At this juncture, let's take a look at the gradients we're going to be using
in Figure E6.8. The blue colors on the right will be used to create the denim
jeans and reds adjacent to them will be the colors for the shirt. Next over are
the three flesh tones and on the other side of the purple are the dark browns
to be used in the hair. For now, we're simply going to use the flood fill tool
to color in our line sprite so it looks like Figure E6.9.

FIGURE E6.9 A filled-in sprite.

Typically, I'll use a color somewhere in the middle of the gradient as a base color—this way I can build up areas of shadow as well as areas of highlight. Alternatively, it is also a fairly common practice to start with the lightest color and build in the shadows from there—which emulates shading with a pencil or a pen. Ultimately it is up to you, but using the middle tone will set you up to easily follow along with the next exercise.

CHAPTER 7

Drawing Secrets Revealed

It's All Smoke and Mirrors

THE CREATION OF GOOD LOOKING ART may seem like magic—and when an artist makes something appear it can certainly feel like sorcery. Of course art is not magic but follows a series of rules that can be taught—much like the principles that govern programming.

Some of the specific rules that make artwork look convincing are shading and cast shadow, light consistency, atmospheric perspective, and linear perspective.

Note to artists: If you are already pretty confident in your art abilities, you are likely to have been exposed to most of the material in this chapter... So I won't be heartbroken if you skip ahead (feckless hooligan). That being said, if you want a refresher or simply enjoy my witty banter—read on!

7.1 SHADING

If you've worked in 3D you may be familiar with the idea of raycasting or normals (although don't freak out if you haven't, I'm trying to connect with my programmer brethren); drawing with shadow is done the same way.

Basically it works like this: Any surface that is perpendicular to a light source reflect back the most light and be the brightest part of an object. As the surface angles becomes closer to 180° (being parallel to the light source), the surface will appear darker. Let's look at Figure 7.1—notice how the plane most closely facing the light source (the top) is lighter and the side facing away from the light source is the darkest.

We can see in Figures 7.1 through 7.3 how changing the relationship of the light source changes the angle that the light hits each surface of the cube. Note how in each case, the surface that most faces the light source is the lightest.

FIGURE 7.1   Surfaces facing the light source will appear lighter.

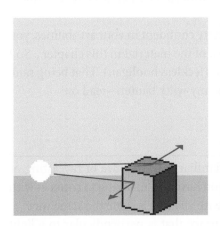

FIGURE 7.2   Light sources don't always come from above.

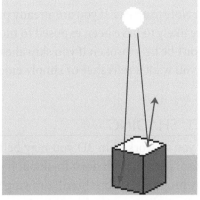

FIGURE 7.3   The angled surfaces reflect differing amounts of light.

This is the major concept that underlies creating the illusion of 3D form in two dimensions. There are other ideas that get used in conjunction but this is the big momma of concepts for drawing form.

For curved forms, the angle of the surface changes in relation to the light source so we use a gradient to represent this, as shown in Figure 7.4.

That wasn't too bad, was it?

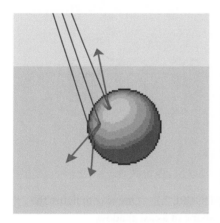 

FIGURE 7.4   Curved surfaces gradually change angle.

FIGURE 7.5   Light can bounce off other surfaces.

Since we've started looking at the lighting of a sphere, I'm just going to give a couple more concepts. Two lighting effects that will often occur on a sphere is a highlight (sometimes called a specular highlight or "spec hit" in game development) and reflected or "bounced" light.

Reflected light is seen when an object gets light from a source other than the primary light source. In the case of Figure 7.5, there is light bouncing off the ground that makes a band at the bottom of the sphere a bit lighter.

A highlight is where this is a high concentration of bright area that reflects off of an object, also seen in Figure 7.5.

One last idea for you to chew on is that all of these examples are built in a neutral gray without much notable texture. In general, objects have various different attributes that affect the way that light bounces off them. Consider how much highlight you would observe on a freshly waxed wood floor compared to a rug. Obviously a wood floor would give a much more acute highlight, and perhaps even a bit of reflection. Don't get bent out of shape with the potential complexity—just be aware that these things exist.

7.2 CAST SHADOW

So keeping the concept of rays of light in mind—if one object is reflecting the ray of light, then those rays will not hit any objects behind. In the case of our cube, we can imagine the rays of light continuing the path to map out where the cast shadow will fall, as done in Figures 7.6 through 7.8.

FIGURE 7.6   The edges of the object block light.

FIGURE 7.7   One way to figure the shape of a cast shadow.

FIGURE 7.8   Cast shadow.

Since the object is bouncing those rays of light, they never reach the surface below and that area will be in shadow. For this reason, it is always supremely important to know where the scene's light source is—at least if you want to create acceptable shadows.

The images with the cube in Figures 7.6 through 7.10 show the step-by-step process of how to figure out where the object's shadow will fall on the ground. In Figure 7.9, we can note how and where the edges of the cube will cast shadow on the ground, and in Figure 7.10, we see the final outcome of our efforts.

FIGURE 7.9 Edges that cast the shadow.

FIGURE 7.10 A cube with shadow.

The idea is straightforward but it can get complicated when dealing with unusual surfaces. Fortunately for us, in most cases we can approximate and the viewer's eye will accept it within the context of the picture.

One last concept in regard to cast shadow is that in real life shadow is not cast uniformly. The shadow is usually darkest close to where the object touches the surface and gets lighter as it gets father away. This is illustrated in Figure 7.11. Also of note is that the edges of a shadow tend to get blurrier as they are farther from the casting object.

FIGURE 7.11 Shadows tend to get blurrier further away.

Many times these aspects of light and shadow are ignored or simplified to make sense within an animation or game development context. There are many times when these ideas simply won't make sense in production—that could be due to file size restraints, time constraints, complexity when animated, or consistency.

But all in all, you are better off understanding the concept of light and shadow and choosing for yourself what you want to exclude or simplify.

7.3 SHADOW DIRECTION

The one thing that the viewer will often *not* accept is when the shadow is outright inconsistent with the light source.

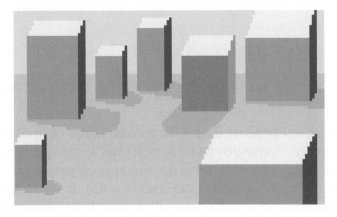

FIGURE 7.12   Which shadow is wrong?

Can you work out which block in Figure 7.12 has inconsistent shading?

It is easy to avoid shading accidents with individual objects but a complicated scene can easily have an item that is inconstant with the rest of the image. Perhaps you've flipped a sprite in your game on the x-axis and the shading direction has changed. It slipped under your radar and looks wrong—much like the second block from the right. The viewer may not know why something looks awkward, but will likely notice that something is off.

These accidents can be avoided fairly easily once you are aware of them. Now you've been warned.

Of course, it may be useful for you to know that we'll be breaking this particular rule on a regular basis. But it is actually fairly important that you understand what light is supposed to do in normal circumstances. This way you can intelligently weigh the tradeoff between visual accuracy and ease of production.

7.4 ATMOSPHERIC PERSPECTIVE

FIGURE 7.13   A city scene.

Let's take a look at Figure 7.13. In particular, I want to break down why the things in the background appear farther away than the things in the foreground.

There are basically three visual concepts that our brains are using to work out the relative distance of objects in the scene: overlapping, size, and atmospheric perspective.

Size works in a fairly familiar way. Put simply, objects appear smaller as they are farther from the viewer.

Overlapping is when an object in the foreground partially covers something behind it. Our brains unconsciously parse this data into depth information. Let's take a look at the building in the center of Figure 7.13. This building is being partially covered by the two buildings in the foreground, dramatically changing the building's profile. Take a look at Figures 7.14 and 7.15 where I've stripped away the foreground buildings so you can see just how different the building's profile becomes when obstructed. Weird, eh?

FIGURE 7.14   Overlapping creates   FIGURE 7.15   Isolated overlap.
depth.

But the primary visual concept I want to talk about is something called atmospheric perspective. This is the fact that objects that are farther away usually appear to be lighter and frequently bluer. Because there is air (atmosphere) between an object and the viewer, these tiny particles layer on top of each other becoming slightly opaque over a long distance.

In Figure 7.16 through Figure 7.19, I've taken Figure 7.13 and broken into a few layers so that we can observe how the buildings in the background become much lighter and bluer as they are farther away.

FIGURE 7.16   Far away things look lighter.

FIGURE 7.17   Closer objects have more detail.

FIGURE 7.18   Objects that are closer have more contrast.

FIGURE 7.19   Closer objects have more saturation.

So slightly shifting the colors used to make your backgrounds can make a huge difference in the feeling of depth within your game.

A wonderful side effect of this process is that it becomes very easy to make the interactive layer of your game stand out boldly to the player—making the game clearer to understand. Even if the background gets complex, it's fairly easy to make the background sit back using atmospheric perspective (as shown in Figure 7.20).

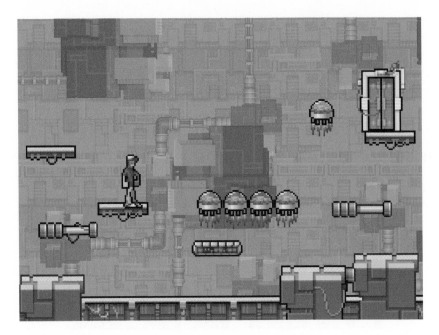

FIGURE 7.20   Even complicated backgrounds can sit back.

7.5 LINEAR PERSPECTIVE

Linear perspective is an expansion of the concept that as things are farther from the viewer, they appear smaller. This is the most common form of perspective used and is usually what is being spoken about if someone mentions "perspective" without context. It is called "linear" perspective because of the explicit technique of figuring out how the size of something is in relation to the scene—using lines to map out the size of objects in the scene. Let's take a look at how to do this:

The first order of business is to establish where the horizon line lies. The horizon line is an imaginary horizontal line in the distance where the ground and the sky meet, as shown in Figure 7.21.

FIGURE 7.21   The horizon line.

The horizon line can appear very low in a picture or very high, and each creates a different viewing experience, as shown in Figure 7.22.

FIGURE 7.22   High and low horizon line.

After creating a horizon line, you will establish a vanishing point at some place on the horizon line. A vanishing point in a place off in the distance where lines that are parallel appear to converge, as shown in Figures 7.23 through 7.26.

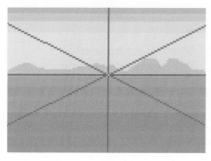

FIGURE 7.23   A vanishing point.

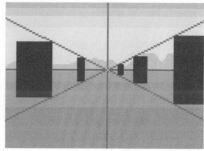

FIGURE 7.24   Using linear perspective to place objects.

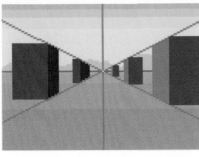

FIGURE 7.25 Vanishing point lines define some of the edges.

FIGURE 7.26 Linear perspective implies object scale.

As you can see, this works remarkably well for buildings and blocks that are all intended to be the same height (and would be better still when atmospheric perspective is used). But what happens when we are dealing with shapes that are of significantly different sizes within the images, such as in Figure 7.27?

Before even figuring out the shapes in the relating blocks, we're going to use atmospheric perspective to make some of these blocks appear closer or farther away. This will make it easier for our eye to accept that there are very large objects in background, such as the block in the upper left. Next, we use imaginary lines to connect the points of the blocks closest to the vanishing point—as shown in Figure 7.28.

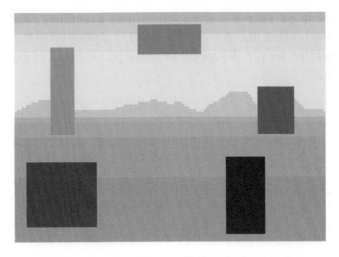

FIGURE 7.27 Objects appearing above and below the horizon line.

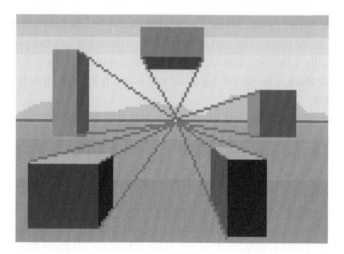

FIGURE 7.28   Using linear perspective to determine scale.

Let's take a closer look at Figure 7.28, as it has some differences from the first linear perspective suite of examples. The bottom two blocks are below the horizon line, so the tops of the blocks are visible. Likewise, the cube in the top-center is above the horizon line, so the bottom of the cube is visible to the viewer.

One more subtle difference seen in the bottom two cubes is that because of their orientation toward the vanishing point, two sides of the cubes can be seen going back into space instead of one. When we take out the guide-lines and add some shadow as in Figure 7.29, we are left with a reasonably convincing image of cubes in a three-dimensional space.

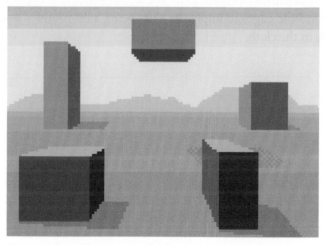

FIGURE 7.29   A reasonably convincing image.

A couple of last points about linear perspective before moving on. In our examples, we've placed the vanishing point in the center of the picture, but this is actually a bit formulaic for my taste and was done more for the ease of demonstration. The vanishing point can actually appear anywhere on the horizon line.

The other thing I wanted to touch on was that it is also possible to use multiple vanishing points within one picture. This can be used to create really nice effects—but is beyond the scope of what I want to cover in this book. A single vanishing point will give you all you need for most game development Pixel Art situations.

Artwork has several consistent properties that can be easily leveraged when you create your work. Shading and cast shadow, light consistency, atmospheric perspective, and linear perspective are all tools that have the potential to give depth to your Pixel Art—both literally and figuratively. You can think of these properties as rules that help the viewers' eyes to understand visual material.

We will be breaking these rules on a regular basis.

EXERCISE 7.1: SHADING THE SPRITE (FROM EXERCISE 6.1)

At this juncture we will use the rules of light discussed in the last chapter to build on our sprite from the earlier exercises.

In Figure E7.1, we have our sprite from before, and he looks quite flat because there is no light or shadow to give depth to the character. The first thing that I'm going to do is too have his enormous head cast a shadow onto his red shirt as shown in Figure E7.2. You'll also notice that I've added a few pixels around the edges to imply the shirt being a bit rounded and having some folds in the cloth.

FIGURE E7.1 Sprite
from the Chapter 6
exercise.

FIGURE E7.2 The head
casts a shadow.

Next I'll start to add some shadow to the face at the bottom and under
the eyes. The hair will also cast some shadow so I'll darken the skin
just below the hairline. I'll add some shadow under the nose and to the
underside of the arms and hands as shown in Figure E7.3.

Now we'll add some light to the thigh area on the pants so that the area
below the shins read as being in shadow. I've also used the darker blue to
create the design of the pocket and seam on the pants, trying to do as much
as I can with only the two colors.

In Figure E7.4, I've added some shadow into the hair and shoes and the
character is starting to appear to have more depth.

FIGURE E7.3 Adding shadow to the pants and skin.

FIGURE E7.4 Even the hair can use some shadow.

FIGURE E7.5 Highlights added to the skin and shirt.

FIGURE E7.6 Highlights added to the hair.

In Figure E7.5, we start to define the features of the face by adding a lighter tone to the skin. Remember from the previous chapter that the various surfaces will get more light as their orientation to the light source gets closer to perpendicular—well this applies to skin too.

The side of the nose and the cheekbones are lightest where they protrude and create surfaces facing the light. The top of the cheekbone and the back of the hands also catch some light that helps to give the appearance of being rounded. We can also add a lighter color red for the parts of the shirt that catch the light. The top of the shoes have been lightened, and the pants get a bit of added shadow.

In Figure E7.6, we have only to add some light into the top most part of the hair and we are done! Good job!

CHAPTER 8

Animating Pixels

The Shock and Horror of Being Flashed by a Pixel

A NIMATION CAN GO A LONG WAY toward creating polish for your game. It can give depth to your characters, personality to your text or environment, and even give subtle clues about the game.

People think of animation not as simply making something move—but technically it is the process of bringing an inanimate object or image alive. As you may know, the illusion of life is given through the quick succession of images that our eyes interpret as movement. We'll only have time to skim over this meaty topic and help to avoid some of the common pitfalls of animating with pixels.

To begin with, allow me to throw out a few pieces of technical information to hold in your brain about animation:

- Traditional animation was done at 24 frames per second; a lower frame rate risks looking "choppy."

- 30 frames per second has become more common today.

- Some current/next generation games run at 60 frames per second to get a super-smooth appearance. We will not be doing that here.

- For video games, the animation of the character or object is typically done in place. For instance, imagine if we had a character walking across the screen; this would be created by creating a cycle of a walking animation done **in place**—and a programming script that would move that sprite across the screen.

I'm going to take a few minutes to show you some of the animation tools in GraphicsGale before launching into the foundation principles of animation. This is so that you will be able to follow along with my descriptions but also to give you an opportunity to experiment on your own a bit.

Every Pixel Art program will have tools similar to things I'll be explaining, but if you are using a different program you'll be on your own to figure out where the appropriate buttons and commands are placed.

8.1 USING THE PROGRAM FOR ANIMATION

The core of animating in pixels will consist of duplicating a frame and making small changes to give the illusion of movement.

In GraphicsGale, this is done by pressing the little down arrow button and then choosing the "duplicate frame" option in the drop-down menu as shown in Figure 8.1. This will activate a second pop up box shown in Figure 8.2. After hitting "OK" there will be a perfect duplicate of the frame shown previously named Copy (the title of the last frame).

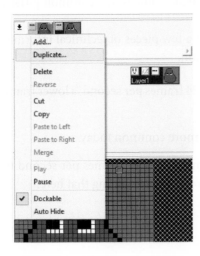

FIGURE 8.1 Duplicate frames to save effort.

FIGURE 8.2 GraphicGale's frame properties.

To move back and forth between frames of animation, simply click on the frame you want to work on in the animation window on the right hand side.

You can also access these tools with buttons that reside at the top of the page shown in Figure 8.3. From left to right the icons in this figure are (1) add frame, (2) the duplicate frame button, (3) delete frame, (4) move backward one frame, (5) move forward one frame, (6) properties of the current frame, (7) cut the current frame (useful for moving to a different place in the sequence), (8) copy the current frame, (9) paste frame from the clipboard, (10) play the animation (in the "Preview" window that can be accessed by checking the appropriate box in the "View" menu drop down), and (11) pause animation.

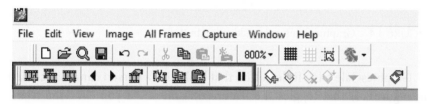

FIGURE 8.3   GraphicGale's animation toolkit.

8.2 ONION SKINNING

Onion skinning is a feature that many programs use to see the frame (or several frames) before and after the frame you are working on. This emulates the quality of working on a light table and helps to project what the movement will look like.

FIGURE 8.4   GraphicGale's onion skinning button.

GraphicsGale has a little button that looks like a person running (circled in Figure 8.4) that toggles the feature on and off. If you click the triangle to the right of the icon, you'll actually find three options: Back Frame, Forward Frame, and Both. This lets you decide whether to look at frames before or after the current frame (or both). It's really quite self explanatory and I'm questioning my judgment as to including that last sentence, as well as this one.

Soliloquy aside, in GraphicsGale there is something else you need to do in order see the onion skin. You need to let GraphicsGale know which color you want to be (semi-)transparent. To do this, we need to click the three little dots on the upper left side of the frame in the animation window (circled in Figure 8.5). This should pop up the "Properties" dialogue box shown in Figures 8.6 and 8.7.

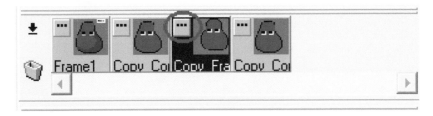

FIGURE 8.5   Frame properties.

FIGURE 8.6   Click the "Transparent: Enabled" checkbox.

FIGURE 8.7   Designate a color to be transparent.

Simply check the "Transparent: Enabled" box and choose the color you want to be semitransparent and violà! You've got a semi for onion skinning!

8.3 PIXEL FLASHING

Pixel flashing is probably the single most troublesome aspect of animating Pixel Art and contrary to your expectations, this is not when a pixel reveals its reproductive parts.

When a pixel or group of pixels suddenly appear or disappear (rather than move position), the appearance can be jarring. Unfortunately, there are times where it may be unavoidable, especially at very low resolutions.

It is somewhat difficult to represent this concept with still images so bear with me as best as you can.

The character on the left in Figure 8.8 has a one pixel gap on the right side where the jaw meets the shoulder, but when he turns his head the gap is filled with a dark pixel. This has the potential to be jarring. Figure 8.9 is even worse; in addition to the gap from before, the line describing the right side of the head has become broken by both light and darker pixels.

Figure 8.10 resolves the issue by keeping the transition as smooth as possible. If you don't see the difference or why this could be troublesome, don't worry—this can be very subtle. This is something extremely difficult to notice when not in motion but I wanted to bring up the concept because it is fairly important for animation. And once you see and understand the issue it becomes very difficult to look past. So please... *please* keep your eyes open for this atrocity.

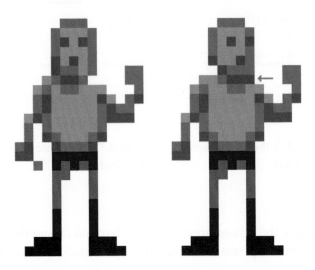

FIGURE 8.8   A single pixel can cause issues in animation.

FIGURE 8.9   Be careful not to make the situation worse.

FIGURE 8.10   A reasonable solution.

8.4 CORE ANIMATION CONCEPTS

Animation is a huge field with many concepts that can be studied—but since this is a book on Pixel Art rather than animation, I've tried to distill it into the most fundamental concepts for making something come alive: anticipation with follow-though, and squash and stretch.

I've made an animorphized red blob to illustrate these ideas (Figure 8.11). He's going to throw his hat with his head.

FIGURE 8.11   An animorphized red blob.

8.4.1 Anticipation and Follow-Through

Anticipation is any motion that gives the viewer a suggestion of what is about to happen. Obvious examples would be of a pitcher winding up to throw a baseball or a boxer pulling his arm back for a strike. In most cases it works quite well to exaggerate this motion as far as possible: not just showing the pitcher pulling her arm back—but pulling her head back, and arcing her entire body in anticipation of the throw.

But in animation it really pays off to use this concept to exaggerate almost any motion: rather than have a character move his arm to pick up a coffee mug—if there is wind up before moving the arm forward—it becomes a more convincing motion.

Our blob is going to throw it's hat to the left—but before it does, it needs to get some head momentum. Although it doesn't really have a head... But our blob does need to lean back in order for the motion to read correctly. Figure 8.12 shows that part of the motion by having the blob lean back to get ready to toss the hat.

FIGURE 8.12   Winding up to throw the hat.

Follow-through is the continuation of the motion after it would otherwise be completed. To extend our examples from earlier: After a pitcher throws the ball, her arm continues to follow that path for a few moments afterward—showing the momentum. Her sleeves and hair fly forward and her weight is extended to the other foot.

In the case of our blob, it's head will continue to extend. The hat will continue its trajectory while the blob settles back into a normal position and the eyes will follow the hat's motion as seen in Figure 8.13. The motion of the hat can be thought of as follow-through, but is also frequently called "secondary animation".

FIGURE 8.13   Follow-through.

Secondary animation refers to the objects that move in reaction to the primary movement of the character. This could be clothing on the character or an item in the environment but could also be part of the character that swings in reaction to the primary movement—such as arms that sway while the character walks.

When we add the anticipation and the follow-through together, the animation looks like Figure 8.14:

FIGURE 8.14   Anticipation and follow-through together.

One more thing I feel I have to address before we move on is when an animation is intended to move very fast. There are times where an object is supposed to move very far in one frame and that motion can be easily lost. Take a look at Figure 8.15. In this figure the ball is on the left side of the picture in one frame and on the right in the next. The ball has to move a great distance in one frame and has the potential to get visually "lost" because our eyes won't be able to fill the missing motion. One way to deal with this is to use ghost versions of the image showing the trail of motion, as shown in Figure 8.16.

FIGURE 8.15   Fast moving objects can get lost between frames.

FIGURE 8.16   Use a trail of motion to avoid losing an object.

In the case of the anamorphic blob, there isn't really a huge distance to cover but if I wanted to really emphasize the speed of the head jerk I could add this effect to one frame of the animation, as shown in Figure 8.17. If you look closely, you can see several different attributes that were added in an attempt to trick the viewers' eyes into reading this as motion. One is the repetition of several lines of the right profile tracking the imaginary motion. Another is a line tracing the path of the motion itself—in this case it would be the lines showing the path of the hat above and below. Lastly, there is the stretching of attributes from one location to the other done with the eyes in this image.

FIGURE 8.17   Using effects to imply fast motion.

When you are creating your animations, consider what sorts of things could use anticipation and follow-through. Although this will add more frames to your animations, the technique will have a huge payoff in the quality of your work. The nice thing about doing this with pixels is that you can often create the effect by literally only moving one or two pixels.

8.4.2 Squash and Stretch

Squash and stretch are almost exactly what they sound like: taking the character (or object or item) and stretching it or squashing it beyond what would be possible in real space. As an abstract idea it is very similar to anticipation and follow-through—they help the idea come alive through exaggeration.

Let's take a look at a jump animation for our blob and how we can use squash and stretch to really make this movement look awesome. In Figure 8.18, we have our character getting ready to jump, which in this case is really a type of anticipation (discussed before). Our blob in now roughly twice the width and half the height as the starting point for the character—this is the "squash" in the expression squash and stretch. Notice that even his hat gets a little squashed which I like, although we're going to revisit how the hat behaves shortly.

FIGURE 8.18 Squash.

Now that our little blobby dude is ready, let's have him spring upward stretching his body in the other direction like in Figure 8.19. This time our blob is roughly twice the height and half the width as the starting point for the character—this is the "stretch." Since the motion is going upward, I've added a change to the brim to emphasize the force of the upward motion.

FIGURE 8.19 Stretch.

What we have looks pretty nice, but let's see how far we can push this concept. Let's really exaggerate the squash and stretch by adding two more frames to pushing the change even farther, like the ones in Figure 8.20.

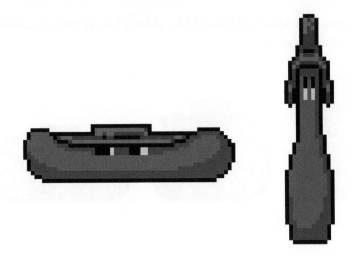

FIGURE 8.20   Exaggerated squash and stretch frames.

While these may look strange and comical as still images, they blend right into the animation and will help to give the impression of an entity that is alive.

One more change that I want to make to this animation is to separate the hat's movement into secondary animation to continue to improve the feel of the movement. In this case we'll have the blob squash so fast that the hat will take a moment to drift back down to the blob's head. To make this work properly we're going to need to take off the squash from the hat. All together with the squash, stretch, and follow-through our jump animation will look like Figure 8.21. You may notice that although we took the squash effect off of the hat so that it can drift down as a secondary animation, the hat still stretches as the character expands upward. You may have to experiment to figure out what works for you and your characters.

FIGURE 8.21   Squash and stretch frames.

I've used a blob to make the point extremely explicit, but in truth this can be used with just about anything, from inanimate objects to on-screen text.

FIGURE 8.22   A typical crappy game animation.

For the sake of the discussion let's imagine that you wanted to have a cannon fire in your game. Figure 8.22 shows what you would frequently see as the animation created for most games. One frame of blast, one frame at rest—that is all. While this is very efficient, there is definitely a missed opportunity for giving that cannon some character. Building games is difficult and time consuming so I fully understand and highly respect keeping things as simple as possible, but animation can genuinely add so much to the players' experience.

So going back to the cannon, we could easily create some anticipation by having a fuse that animates before the firing, as in Figure 8.23. This has the potential to be an interactive/gameplay element as well, creating a delay between the command and the desired effect—but for now I simply want to use it as a seven-frame agent of anticipation.

FIGURE 8.23   Anticipation has been created.

Figure 8.24 creates a climax for the anticipation with a squash, squishing the object horizontally and extending it vertically. I've squashed both the barrel and the wheels, but feel to experiment because squashing different parts will give a different feel to the animation. It doesn't really matter that the object is made of iron—it still has a very appealing aesthetic, creating some life in an otherwise static object.

FIGURE 8.24 Squash can be added to inanimate objects.

Figure 8.25 uses some stretch to really emphasize the blast. The animation places the most squashed frame right next to the most stretched frame, creating a lot of contrast—which is perfect for something like a cannon blast. This is followed by some secondary animation of the smoke settling and the cannon slightly rolling back (which you cannot really see in the still image other than the wheel rolling a bit).

FIGURE 8.25 Stretch and follow through.

All put together, Figures 8.22 through 8.24 create a cannon that doesn't just shoot, but really comes alive when fired. Not too shabby for an inanimate object.

Squash and stretch, anticipation and follow-through, and secondary animation are really only the tip of the iceberg for animation technique. There is so much more to be explored from timing to lip synching to posture and gesture, that I really could not possibly cover everything here.

The best I can hope for is to give you a taste and strongly encourage you to explore the craft further.

8.5 GAME-SPECIFIC CONCERNS

Soon we'll try our hand at creating a little animation but before getting started on that exercise, it is worthwhile to touch on some components of animation that are specific to games. There are fundamental differences between animation for games versus animation for film or television.

In more traditional animation settings, animations can be entirely built for the context. That is to say that the characters are typically animated to do anything they happen to be doing in the scene—whether it is something very common and repetitive or a movement that is small and unique. A character's movement can then be a continuous motion, with fluid transitions throughout all actions.

Games aren't typically built that way. Because character movements are generally triggered by something the player or environment does dynamically, it is next to impossible to know a character's every movement state necessary in the game. Historically there have also been space restrictions that also limit the amount of assets that a game can hold in memory.

The way that games deal with this is by slicing the movement into individual actions that can be (but aren't always) looped. These tend to be the actions that are done most frequently and in many cases transition animations or non-essential movements are eliminated.

Often games will include the following individual animations:

- A walk cycle

- A run cycle

- An idle animation (activated when no buttons are pressed)

- Attack animations

- Death animation(s)

- A jump

Sometimes the gameplay is augmented by additional animations such as

- A landing animation (when a jump is finished)

- A dance or emotive animation

- Crouching/crawling

- Taking damage

- Climbing

- Pulling out weapon

- Waving arms to catch balance

These can be triggered by a player pressing a button (such as an attack) or by an interaction of the environment (such as taking damage).

In most cases it is difficult to account for all transitions between movements within a game and often animations "snap" from one to the next. This usually works just fine within the context of game and players generally have the expectation that their character will respond with immediate feedback.

This is a very good thing because it would be very challenging to create transition animations between all of the main animations. Consider that I have listed 13 animations listed earlier in my noncomprehensive list. If my math is correct, and it probably is *not*—in order to have transitions between all of these you would need create 144 animations to create all possible transitions!

One more thing to consider for your animations is the number of frames that you'll need to create the animation. A walk cycle animation is frequently done with 8 frames, but could be done with 16 to get a silky-smooth flow of movement. I've also seen walk cycles created with 2 or 3 frames that give just barely enough information to slip by as a walking movement.

8.6 SUMMARY

We covered how to get started animating in GraphicsGale, using onion skinning to view the adjacent frames for reference. We talked about the dreaded pixel flash and covered a few core animation concepts, including squash and stretch, as well as anticipation and follow-through.

I've tried my best to give you the most fundamental aspects of animating with pixels but animation has its own history and the discipline is too vast to cover in this one section. If you like the idea and want to learn more, I encourage you to pick up a copy of the book *The Animator's Survival Kit* by Richard Williams.

EXERCISE 8.1: CREATE AN IDLE ANIMATION (FROM EXERCISE 7.1)

In the last exercise we covered the basic fundamental aspects of animation. This chapter we will just lightly touch on these by creating a very simple animation—less for putting the foundational aspects into action and more to get accustomed to what it is like to animate with Pixel Art. We'll give a bit of life to this character by creating an idle animation, giving you a couple of possible variations to choose from.

Simplify the Sprite (Suggested but Optional)

Our character has a bit of shading and detail, which is nice, but has the potential to be a real pain to animate. In many cases, you'll want to simplify the sprite as much as possible before creating animations.

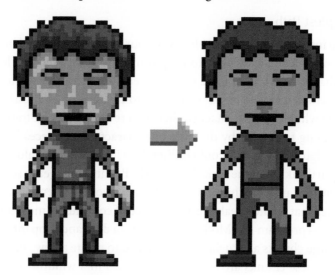

FIGURE E8.1   Simplifying sprite for animation.

Figure E8.1 shows a simplified version of our sprite from earlier—which is probably the first thing I'd do if I were going to create a whole suite of animations for this character. I've eliminated as much detail as I could get away with and reduced the gradients for each hue to no more than two colors.

Why? Why take something that looks nice and strip away detail?

For your sanity!

The more complexity a character has, the more time it will take to create consistent and believable animations. Consider that each bit of detail has to move in proper speed and proportion to the rest of the sprite. What's more, each bit of texture has the potential for creating pixel flash or other jarring artifacts when in motion.

Take a look at the characters created by the great 2D animators throughout history and you'll notice that they tend to be somewhat simple and/or stylized. The best animators know that what they give up in terms of visual complexity they can more than make up for with the quality of movement.

One thing I'd like to point out that was done in this example was to make one arm and one leg entirely in shadow. While this doesn't appear to be a noteworthy change, this actually serves utility when it's time to animate.

This helps to keep clear which limb is the right and which limb is on the left. While this may not seem to make a difference from the front, if the character is facing sideways (as it would be in a side-scrolling game)—having one limb in shadow can be very useful in determining which is which.

The Simplest Path

But if you insist on keeping complexity in your sprite design, I will introduce a couple of ideas that will help to keep things painless. Well... at least less painful than it could be. If we're going to keep our character sprite shaded as it was before, it should be our goal to try to create as much life as possible by moving whole sections intact (rather than re-drawing each frame).

We're going to do this by dividing our character into pieces like what's shown in Figure E8.2 which could be literal (as I've done) or could be simply the way you think about the sprite figuratively. By thinking of each section as a whole unit, we can move things in "chunks" and avoid accidentally changing the textures that would break the appearance of continuous movement.

Cosmigo's program Pro Motion actually has a drag and drop interface for treating large chunks as brushes, allowing you to create a new "brush" with one click. These chunks are then easily accessed in a window on the side, which can be very helpful throughout the animation process. But because most of you are using GraphicsGale, you can consider placing the various chunks onto different layers.

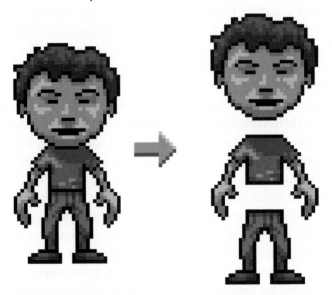

FIGURE E8.2   For complicated sprites, animate in sections.

One of the idiosyncrasies of animating with pixels is that each movement must be at least one pixel distance. While that may not seem like much, it may actually be a large portion of the thing that you are moving. Say you want the character to lift his foot slightly—the foot is only three pixels tall. The smallest distance it can move would be a third of its size, which is not trivial if you are trying to create subtlety. And as a general rule, idle animation tends to be subtle. Hang on tight.

Our most simple iteration of an idle animation would be a simple two-frame cycle where the chest heaves slightly. In this case, the head and the legs stay static, but the torso and arms shift one pixel upward to give the illusion of breathing.

Figure E8.3 shows these two frames that look so similar that I've used an extra image to diagram which pixels actually shifted position. The entire torso was moved in one big chunk, changing only a few pixels at the bottom of the shirt to change the appearance of the creases.

As simple as this animation is, it gives a bit of life to the character when not in action. It seems to work well with a pretty low frame rate, somewhere around 2 frames/second (or 500 milliseconds per frame).

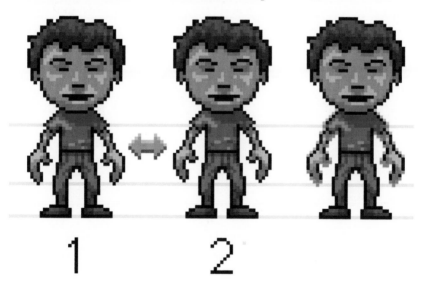

FIGURE E8.3   A movement of 1 pixel is enough to create idle animation.

This actually isn't bad and would work quite well for many games. As slight as the movement may be, it breathes a bit of life into an otherwise static character.

CHAPTER 9

Tiled Backgrounds

IN THIS CHAPTER we'll talk about one of the ways in which Pixel Artists can leverage their effort is by using sections of art over and over again. By creating individual "tiles" that fit together, it becomes easy to cover a huge environment with components that can be arranged an rearranged ad nauseam (apparently the term ad nauseam comes from the concept that something can be discussed until it makes you nauseous—but we'll stop before you get sick, I promise).

Figure 9.1 shows how five 16 × 16 tiles can be reused over and over to make an entire image.

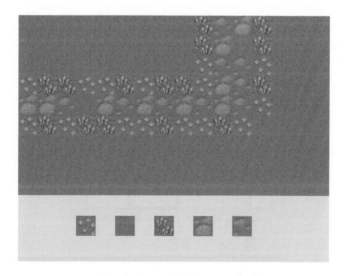

FIGURE 9.1   Several small sections can create a whole scene.

This process gets more mileage from the initial effort, saves computer memory, and gives tools to make the construction of a level very fast. The reusable sections of art are called *tiles* and are kept together in one place called a *tile set*.

9.1 TILE SIZES

A tilemap will be made of tiles that are each the same size. The most common tile sizes are 16×16 pixels, 8×8 pixels, or 32×32 pixels (Figure 9.2).

Notice that the dimensions are all to the power of 2—this allows the computer to deal with the image files more effectively and avoids needlessly wasting computer memory.

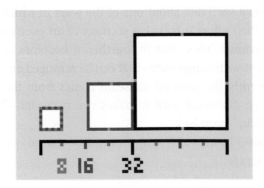

FIGURE 9.2   Tiles are typically built to the power of two.

Another important thing to note is that as the numbers in the dimension size double, the actual amount of space quadruples. Figure 9.3 shows how four 16 × 16 squares fit into one 32 × 32 square.

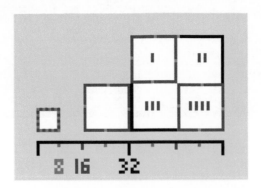

FIGURE 9.3   One 32 × 32 tile can hold *four* 16 × 16 tiles.

This becomes extremely important when considering what size to work in and how much time it will take to build things. Imagine you're working with someone who wants you to build an environment but doesn't really care what size you build the tiles. Figures 9.4 and 9.5 show how a resolution of 32 × 32 will be *16 times* the size of a tile set built at 8 × 8.

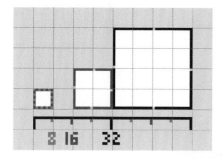

FIGURE 9.4   Compare the size of the 8 × 8 tile to the 32 × 32 tile.

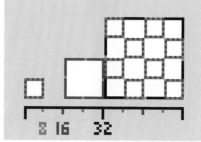

FIGURE 9.5   One 32 × 32 tile can hold *sixteen* 8 × 8 tiles.

This is not only important for keeping the aesthetic consistent and having a quality resolution—but also entirely game changing when managing your work flow and effort. . . and sanity.

I desperately want for you to avoid accidentally agreeing to four times the effort (or more) because you arbitrarily agreed to make sprites and/or environments at a certain size.

9.2   SETTING UP THE TILEMAP WORK AREA

When using tiles, it will be important to display a grid, and useful to toggle the "snap to grid" function. In GraphicsGale, the button to toggle the grid on and off is shown in Figure 9.6. In this screenshot the canvas is only 128 × 128 and this is probably smaller than what I would recommend for a building area if building a tile set that uses 32 × 32 tiles. The size of your canvas should be large enough to make a few rows and columns to test out the tiles you build. So this would probably be a fine size for 16 × 16 tiles—but for the 32 × 32 tile set we'd probably want a canvas to work on that was sized at least 256 × 256.

The grid size should be the size of the tile you're working with for the most part.

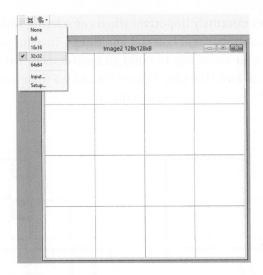

FIGURE 9.6   Work on a grid when creating tiles.

Conveniently, the button to toggle the grid snap function is just to the right of the button that toggles the grid visibility, red circled in Figure 9.7. In truth, this is such a commonly used tool that I would strongly recommend giving it a hotkey. As a reminder, you can set hotkeys in the **File—Preferences** menu under the Key tab. I typically use the character "g" as the hotkey—as g for grid is fairly easy to remember.

FIGURE 9.7   Snap to grid.

9.3 TEXTURES THAT REPEAT ON YOU

There are many instance where an image repeats over and over again like a visual loop—like a brick wall or grass field. This is called an infinitely tiling texture and is one of the places where Pixel Art shines brightest!

In most cases the tile will be repeating both horizontally and vertically so they will have to link up nicely in all directions.

The general composition of a tiling texture tile should be fairly homogenous, as anything that stands out too much will become very obvious when repeating. Following are some examples of things that can adversely affect an infinitely tiling texture, each demonstrated with an example. It's in your best interest to try to avoid the following:

- Elements that stick out too much, like a single rock (Figure 9.8). Although this may be a fine looking tile on its own, once the tile is repeated it totally breaks the illusion of a continuous believable surface.

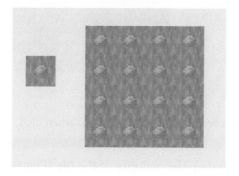

FIGURE 9.8   Some items stick out when tiled.

- Gradients on the tile (Figure 9.9). Gradients are super useful in general, but for the most part they do not work as repeatable tiles.

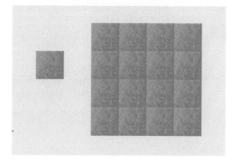

FIGURE 9.9   Gradients create patterns when repeated.

- Dramatic shadows or too much contrast (Figure 9.10). Although this doesn't always break the cycling pattern, it will almost always detract from the scene overall. Contrast will bring attention to the tile, making it harder to hide the repetition. It also causes a situation where the main subjects—such as the character—fight for priority with the environment, which is not desirable.

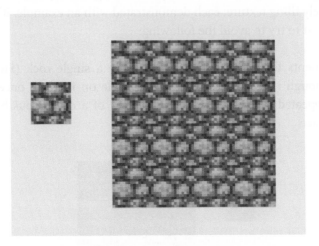

FIGURE 9.10   High contrast can create problems when tiled.

- One item taking up the majority of the tile (Figure 9.11). This makes the repetition of the tiles painfully obvious.

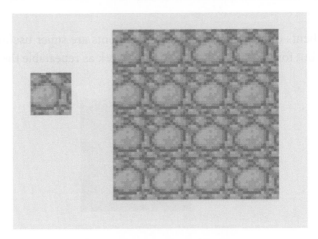

FIGURE 9.11   Some patterns stick out when repeated.

- Tight concentration of detail in only part of the tile (Figure 9.12). This creates an effect similar to having something take up the majority of the tile—and the repetition once again becomes obvious.

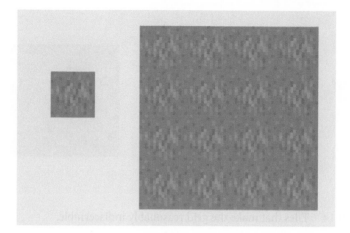

FIGURE 9.12   Concentrated patterns become conspicuous when repeated.

- Accidentally emphasizing the tile edge (Figure 9.13). Avoid putting too many pixels in a row right on the edges of the tile and you run the risk of popping that tile out.

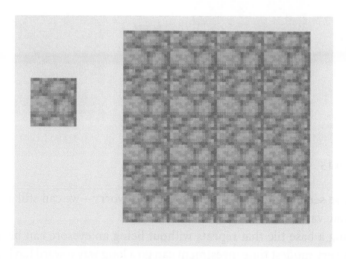

FIGURE 9.13   Avoid making the grid too obvious.

Now compare those against these tiles (Figure 9.14). It is not that the aesthetic is so much better with these two, but the fact that they are being repeated over and over becomes greatly obscured.

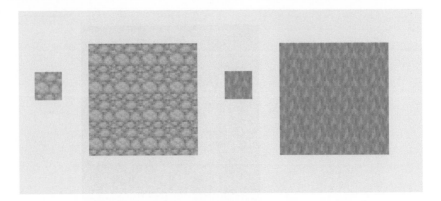

FIGURE 9.14   Tiles that make the grid reasonably indiscernible.

Although there are times when emphasizing the tile works in your favor. An example would be when you want to represent something angular or ridged. Or perhaps there may be a time where you need to represent tiles (such as floor tiles) with your tiles (Figure 9.15).

FIGURE 9.15   Sometimes a noticeable grid is okay.

If these seem a bit too bland for you, don't worry—we can still add tiles that create variation!

Having a base tile that repeats without being an eyesore can be a huge asset. A very modest time investment can go a long way toward having your game look appealing—even in early prototype phases!

Once your infinitely tiling texture is created and you feel good about it, you can add variations to make it look more organic and generally more aesthetically interesting. When we take simple repeating textures and add just a few variation tiles, it immediately becomes more interesting (Figure 9.16).

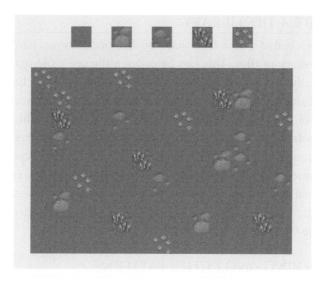

FIGURE 9.16   Use variation tiles to break the monotony.

And once those are built, we can use these elements to imply a path and start to guide gameplay like in Figure 9.17.

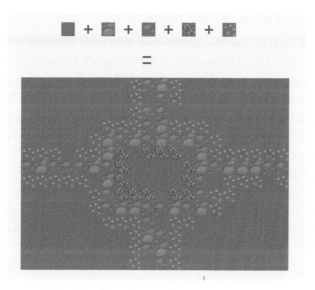

FIGURE 9.17   Variation tiles can compose your environment.

9.4 CREATE A TILE LIBRARY

Once you've created a few tiles that you feel good about, you'll want to keep a repository of tiles. This can be called a tile set, a tile map, or a tile palette. It really doesn't matter what you call it, although it is helpful to keep it organized and up to date as your tiles change and improve over time.

Some Pixel Art programs such as Pro Motion and Pyxel Edit have some advanced tools that go a long way toward making the process easier. Specifically what comes to mind is the autoupdate feature that allows you to make changes to one tile and the program automatically updates all of the same tile type in real time. This can be super helpful in eliminating the seam when creating tiling textures. Unfortunately to the best of my knowledge, at this point in time GraphicsGale does not have this feature.

9.5 DITHERING AND OTHER PATTERNS

Dithering is the concept of using the placement of pixels to imply blending between colors. Because Pixel Art typically uses a limited palette, dithering can trick the viewer into perceiving more colors than are actually used.

I think about dithering as having two main categories: patterned and organic. In most cases I prefer an organic dither, so we'll start with that one.

9.5.1 How to Create Organic Dither

Put a tile of each of the two colors that you want to blend next to each other (I've used a 16 × 16 sized tile in my example). Dithering can easily be completed using a two-step process, although other methods exist. Figure 9.18 shows the process and follows the steps explained in the following:

Step 1: Add pixels of one color into the other side. Make the concentration more dense as it gets closer to the barrier between the two colors. Try to avoid static patterns (we'll talk about those shortly), but try to place the pixels quasirandomly.

Step 2: Repeat the process with the other color, going the other direction.

The end result is a gradient that appears to blend from one color into the next. This kind of dither works very well for creating skies, shadows, and other sorts of organic shading.

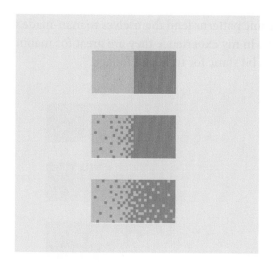

FIGURE 9.18   Organic dithering.

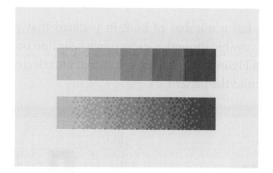

FIGURE 9.19   Dithering can imply blending.

Figure 9.19 shows how a gradient that has been dithered appears more blended—or at least the blend has a softer appearance.

9.5.2 Patterned Dither

Patterns can be another handy tool for creating blending on less organic items. The most commonly used of these is the standard checkerboard pattern shown in the middle of Figure 9.20. As you can see in the top part of the figure, there are only five distinct colors being used but the dithering gives the impression to the casual observer that there are nine colors.

Other sorts of patterns can be used separately or conjunction as shown on the bottom of Figure 9.20.

These inorganic patterns lend themselves to man-made textures such as metal or plastic. In my experience they are great for inanimate objects but tend to appear a bit static for trees and foliage.

FIGURE 9.20   Dithering patterns will soften edges in different ways.

GraphicsGale has a number of built-in patterns that you can use for dither built in accessible through a drop-down selection box in the **Palette** menu—shown in Figure 9.21. The two colors that are selected will create the two colors that build the pattern.

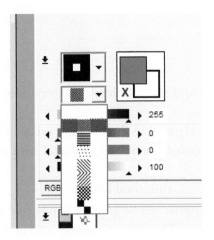

FIGURE 9.21   Default dithering patterns in GraphicsGale.

I've occasionally seen people dither with elaborate hand drawn patterns that can be very stylized and striking. Experiment and decide what works best for you.

One last note on dithering: animation and dither are mortal enemies, mix them at your own peril. Because of pixel flash and the potential for texture inconsistency, this combination is fraught with problems. This is not a challenge—if you can pull it off, great... But I do advise against it and would guess that you will need a truckload of aspirin by the time your project is completed.

EXERCISE 9.1: CREATING A TOP-DOWN TILE SET

In the last chapter we talked about how we can use a small set of tiles in a clever way to create a full-sized 2D game environment, as shown in Figure E9.1 example.

While we still have tiled backgrounds fresh in our mind, let's go ahead and build an entire tile set!

I've always had a sweet spot for top-down environments. Growing up in the Nintendo Entertainment System era, this convention was indelibly engraved on my gaming experiences. Games like The Legend of Zelda, Ikari Warriors, Spy Hunter, Final Fantasy I, and Crystalis have become foundational for the top-down aesthetic that is still used today.

But talk is cheap, so let's get started!

Step 1: Create a New Project, Get a History Lesson

Go to **File—New** or hit Ctrl+N to create a new file and we're going to make the dimensions quite a bit bigger than anything we've done so far. We want to make sure that we have room to both draw the individual tiles, but also to place them into a scene to see whether they work within a context.

Let's make this file 256 × 128 pixels with 8-bit color as shown in Figure E9.1.

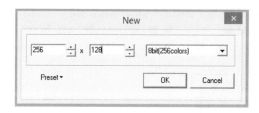

FIGURE E9.1   Create a new file.

Notice that 256 and 128 are both numbers that are a power of 2 (2^8 and 2^7, respectively), which means that the canvas can be tiled evenly with tiles that are each sized at 16×16 or 32×32. We will be using 16×16 tiles for this exercise.

Although we are going to use a 256-color palette, we are actually only going to be using only 32 colors to make our scene. In truth, the idea of an 8-bit palette being 256 colors is a bit misleading (at least as it had been used historically in games). Even though a game's background environment could use all 256 colors in total, each individual tile could use only 16 colors—and frequently one of those colors was reserved for transparency. For this reason, the building of almost any individual object in 8-bit games was restricted to only 16 colors rather than 256.

Since the birth of Pixel Art, the tools available for game development have exploded in scope and accessibility and the hardware being used to run them have become exponentially more powerful. The technical requirements have changed dramatically and we are seldom bound by these restrictions that birthed the style. Since the development scene has changed so dramatically, I've adjusted the instruction accordingly. I've tried my best to create this exercise to give you a solid understanding of the method while avoiding the technical minutia.

Step 2: Turn on Your Grid

When working on a tile-based environment, feeling comfortable with the grid will be key to speed, efficiency, and your sanity. To turn your grid on in GraphicsGale, simply select the grid icon from the toolbar and select the 16×16 option shown in Figure E9.2. To turn off the grid, you would choose None from that same dropdown menu.

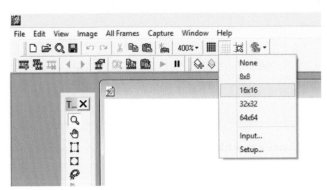

FIGURE E9.2   Turn on the grid.

Also of great importance is the tool just to the left of the grid icon. The icon shown in Figure E9.3 snaps everything to the grid. This is used so frequently that it is a good idea to create a hotkey for this tool in the **File—Preferences** menu. I've assigned the "g" button as my hotkey as you can see in Figure E9.4.

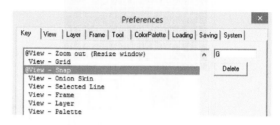

FIGURE E9.3   Snap to grid button.

FIGURE E9.4   Create a "snap to grid" hotkey.

Step 3: Prepare Your Palette

A number of these steps are covered in Chapter 4, but are iterated here for those of you that like to jump right to the tutorials. That being the case, feel free to skip ahead if that makes sense for you.

Your new canvas will have a palette that looks something like the one shown in Figure E9.5. I find it helpful to make the colors I'm working with stand out dramatically from the unused ones. I use black or very dark colors that can be confused with black from time to time, so I prefer to change all unused colors to a bright magenta or neon green. I'm going to use the color third from the right on the bottom (which happens to be 0xFF00FF for those of you that care).

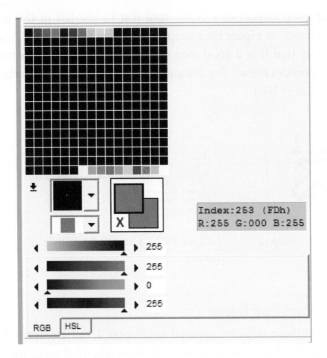

FIGURE E9.5   Default 128 color palette.

FIGURE E9.6   Example of a color ramp.

A "ramp" or "gradient" is a smooth transition between two colors, and in the Pixel Art that would be a set of colors that smoothly transition from one color to the next like what's shown in Figure E9.6.

And we will create a gradient of green like the one shown above, but first we are going to use the same technique in the program to turn the palette all magenta. We're going to copy the magenta, paste it in two places, then "ramp" the two colors together. Because there is no variance between the two colors, it will make a ramp of only one color.

If you haven't done so already, you'll need to assign a hot key to the procedures that we'll need:

- We'll need to copy the color, so in **File—Preferences** menu, find Palette—Copy RGB Value and assign it the C key as shown in Figure E9.7.

- Next, assign the V key to the Palette—Paste RGB Value on the line below as shown in Figure E9.8.

- Finally, we'll assign the R key to the Palette—Make Gradation line, as shown in Figure E9.9.

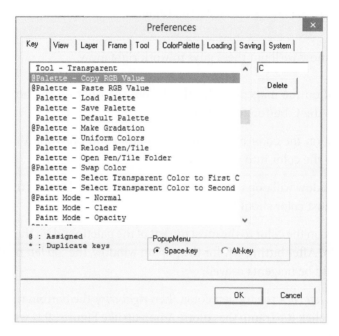

FIGURE E9.7   Set hotkey for "Copy RGB Value."

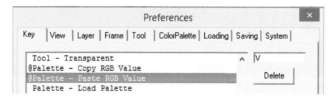

FIGURE E9.8   Set hotkey for "Paste RGB Value."

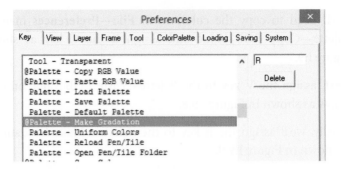

FIGURE E9.9   Set hotkey for "Make Gradation."

Great—now we'll put these guys to work right away.

- Click on the magenta color third from the right on the bottom and press the C button to copy the color.

- Click on the color on the far right bottom and press the V button to paste the color into that position.

- A window will pop up that looks like Figure E9.10. Hit OK (the bottom leftmost color should turn magenta).

- Click on the color to the most top left of the palette and hit the V button again. After hitting OK for the pop up window, the top left most color should be magenta as well.

- Now *left click* the top left color, then *right click* the bottom right color, then click R to ramp the colors. A pop up like Figure E9.11 will pop up. Hit OK.

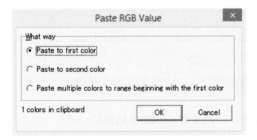

FIGURE E9.10   Copy a color to a new location.

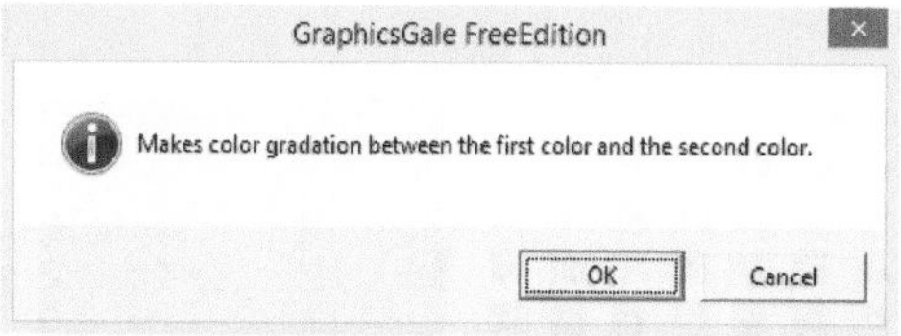

FIGURE E9.11   Create gradation.

If everything worked as it should, your entire palette should be an ugly shade of magenta, as shown in Figure E9.12.

We're going to start our tile-based environment with a grass texture, so let's begin by building a gradient of greens, similar to what's shown in Figure E9.6.

Double click on the second color slot and that should pull up a Color menu. Create the lightest green for our grass by adjusting the sliders until you have something similar to what's seen in Figure E9.13. After hitting OK, you will be left with a light green in the second palette position, like Figure E9.14.

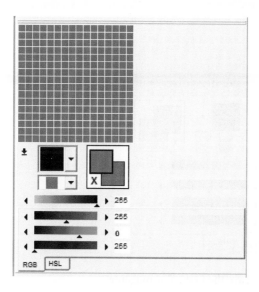

FIGURE E9.12   A clean palette to begin working.

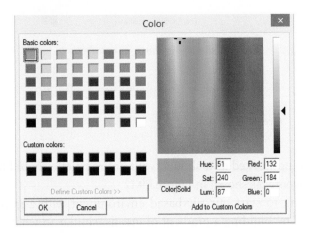

FIGURE E9.13   Choose a neutral green.

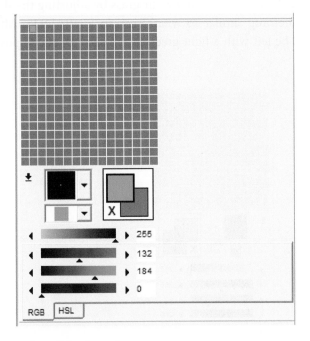

FIGURE E9.14   Leave the first color magenta.

And since we're going to create a seven color gradient like Figure E9.6, we're going to make our darkest grass color several spaces over in the eighth color position. Then we'll ramp the colors together as shown in Figure E9.15.

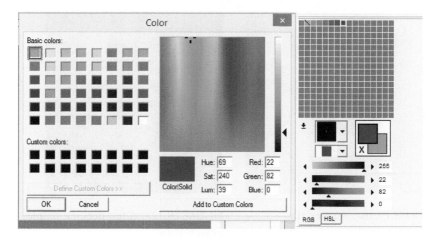

FIGURE E9.15   Pick the darkest green and create a gradient.

You may have noticed that I've left the first color magenta. This is a habit from the old days of creating palettes for low-powered hardware. This is commonly the space that is reserved for transparency. Although this may not be necessary for this particular exercise, it is a useful habit.

With our palette neatly organized, we're now ready to get grooving on creating some artwork!

Step 4: Create Our First Tile

We're going to use our filled rectangle tool to fill in one square of your grid with the middle color of green gradient so it looks like Figure E9.16. As a Pixel Artist you will live and die by the grid, so get used to being conscious of where things fall in relation to the grid.

For our first tile, we're going to keep everything simple and avoid adding complexity for as long as possible. So for our first grass texture, we can start by just adding dots of color at quasirandom places on the square as shown in Figure E9.17.

FIGURE E9.16   A green tile.

FIGURE E9.17   A few dots = a simple grass texture.

I say quasirandom because there actually is a bit of thought to where those little dots are going... Or to be more accurate, where they are not going. For textures that will be repeated over and over again, it is important that nothing stands out too much.

Because grass is an organic entity, it is imperative that the pattern of pixels doesn't read as static. To achieve this, we need to avoid having pixels that line up horizontally or vertically. Take a look at Figure E9.18a, where the tile on the left is being repeated on the right. You can see that the tile has a number of places where the pixels line up. This sort of pattern may work well for manmade materials like plastic or metal, but looks too patterned for organic material like grass.

On the flip side, we also need to avoid making areas of the tile that are too clustered. If there is a higher concentration of pixels in one area of the tile, it will stand out as an intentional pattern once the tile is repeated. We can see this effect in Figure E9.18b. This is almost never desirable in repeating textures although it can work well for accent tiles that create variation.

We want a somewhat uniform distribution of pixels throughout the tile.

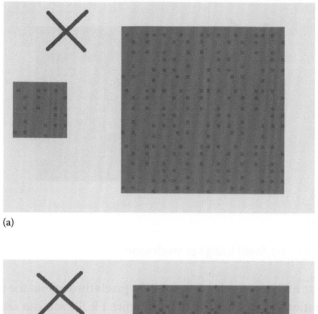

(a)

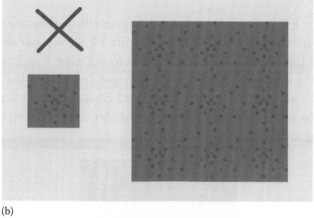

(b)

FIGURE E9.18 (a) Pixels that line up don't look organic. (b) Pixels that cluster don't look organic.

The color being used for the individual dots is the green that is just darker than the middle green and soon we'll add one more color that is a shadow lighter to add some variation. For the most part, we want a fairly low contrast combination of colors for your environments. This serves the function of keeping the backgrounds sitting back so that they won't compete with the character sprites for attention and also helps to keep a repeating tile from looking too patterned. In Figure E9.18c, I've given an example of using too high of a contrast in the tiles colors.

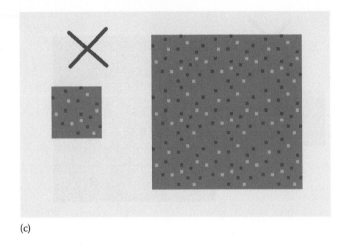

(c)

FIGURE E9.18   (c) Avoid using too much contrast.

In Figure E9.19, I've added in some light pixels throughout the tile to add more variation throughout the tile. In Figure E9.20, you can see that I've duplicated this tile nine times on the grid to see what it looks like when tiled. For the most part this tile looks pretty good when tiled but I'm going to be a little anal retentive and make a small change—in part because it is our first tile, and in part just to illustrate the sort of critical eye you should be working to build.

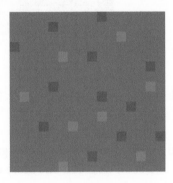

FIGURE E9.19   A seemingly organic grass tile.

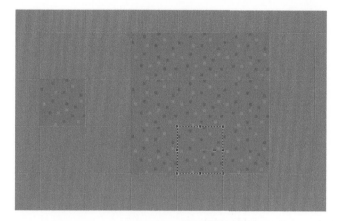

FIGURE E9.20   Duplicate to see how the overall pattern.

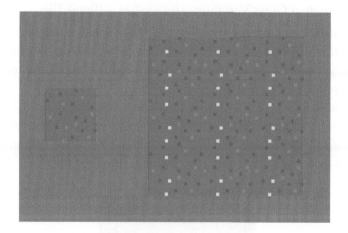

FIGURE E9.21   Some pixels are still lining up.

My eye is picking out a bit of a vertical pattern with a few of the pixels when the tile is repeated, which I've highlighted in Figure E9.21. I'll iterate that I'm being very nitpicky here, but if you notice something like this and you have the time to fix it (and that is often a big *if*) then why not? So I've done a small adjustment so that we end up with what we see in Figure E9.22. Nice.

FIGURE E9.22   A reasonable solution.

Step 5: Create a Grass Variation—As well as a Blend Tile

Congratulations on making your first tile! We're going to follow up by creating a bit of variation in the grass—some areas where it grows a bit more wild. We've been taking it a little slow but we will ramp up the speed of our creation process as we move ahead.

First, let's draw a new tile using the same colors but has a higher concentration of both the light and darker color green, like what's shown in Figure E9.23. For this one, it's okay to have clumps of color—although you still want to keep it fairly evenly distributed throughout the tile.

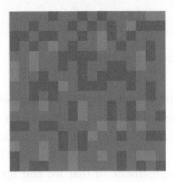

FIGURE E9.23   More going on for a rougher texture.

If you take a look at Figure E9.24, you'll notice that I am keeping both tiles separated over to the left. This is the beginning of a tile bank or tile set, where you'll keep individual copies of each tile you've created.

This new tile looks pretty good but when I tile it, I see a bit of vertical and horizontal alignment that displeases me highlighted in Figure E9.25.

FIGURE E9.24   Duplicate to see how the overall pattern.

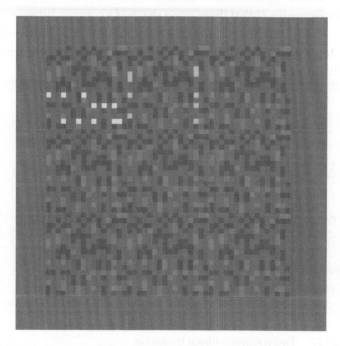

FIGURE E9.25   Some pixels lining up vertically and horizontally.

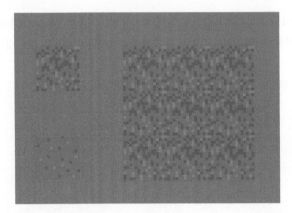

FIGURE E9.26   Good enough!

So after making some adjustments we have what you see in Figure E9.26. The tile is still not really perfect, but quite adequate for our purposes.

As individual textures, these are looking pretty good, but when we start to put those tiles together into a scene we notice a pretty big problem. We can see in Figure E9.27 that there is too sharp of a contrast between the two tiles. On closer look, they actually look okay on the border between left and right or top and down, but the angles look far too blocky for something organic like grass.

FIGURE E9.27   Two textures without transition.

One of the traditional ways to handle this is to make two new tiles to round out the edges, as shown in Figure E9.28 leaving us with two new tiles as shown in Figure E9.29 but that is not really my recommendation. As we can see in Figure E9.30, it definitely cures the angular edges between the grass types, but the curves seem too perfect for organic matter. Another common way to do this is to use what they call a "9 slice"—which we will do later but not for this transition.

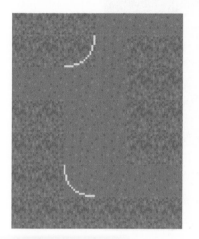

FIGURE E9.28   Creating tiles to round the edges.

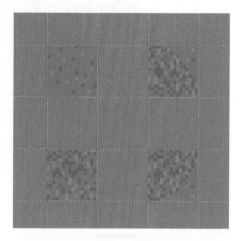

FIGURE E9.29   Two texture tiles and two transition tiles.

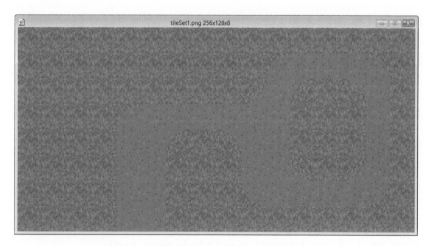

FIGURE E9.30   The edges of the path are now rounded.

Instead, my preference would be to create one tile that makes a softer blend on a diagonal like what's shown in Figure E9.31. This makes the transition a bit softer and also has the advantage of using one less tile to receive a similar effect. Less is more when it comes to Pixel Art. Now we have three tiles, and a satisfactory "blend tile" between the two grasses—all of which can be observed in Figure E9.32.

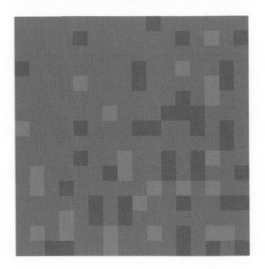

FIGURE E9.31   One tile that will replace the two transition tiles.

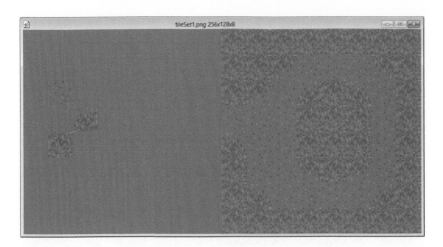

FIGURE E9.32   Less to keep track of and it looks more organic.

Step 6: It Isn't Easy Being Green—Moving on to Sand

In this step, we are going to create a sand tile, then show how to create a "9 slice" to transition between grass and sand using eight tiles. Finally, we'll address another way to handle this issue using only three tiles (which is my preference in most contexts).

First and foremost, we need to add some colors to our palette. My palette is shown in Figure E9.33, which I'll take a moment to explain.

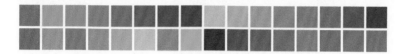

FIGURE E9.33   Our palette with some spots left for emergency.

The gradient of green will be used to create grass, trees, and shrubbery. The gray colors to the right will be used for stones, stone walls, and/or cement. On the bottom row I have a four-color gradient of blue that will be used to create water. Flanking the blue on either side is yellow and purple that I plan to use for flowers (and the blue may get used as well). Then, we've gotten to the brown, which will be used for sand, and perhaps tree trunk or mud. Lastly, there are three spots that are left over that I am leaving as magenta. These can be in reserve if we decide that we really need another color to make something work.

Okay, with our palette squared away, let's build a tile for some sand. In Figure E9.34, I've shown the simple process of creating a sand tile: Begin with a brown tile. (I'm using the lightest brown in my palette.) Then draw some pixels that are grey, but with a similar value to the brown. That is to say, a gray that is roughly the amount of brightness as brown—these are pebbles in the sand. Next we'll add a few places where the pebbles are reflecting a bit of light by adding some lighter color gray dots. Lastly, we'll add some variation in the brown by adding some pixels of brown that are a shade darker.

FIGURE E9.34   Create a generic sand tile.

FIGURE E9.35   We need some transition from grass to sand.

As you can see in Figure E9.35, the sand will need some work in order to integrate properly with the grass. The most common way to deal with this transition is to use a "9-slice."

Essentially a 9 slice is when you create a transition for each of the eight sides that border a tile. You can see in Figure E9.36a through d, I've gone through the steps involved in creating those transitions. In Figure E9.36a, I've outlined the shape that the transition from grass to sand will take. In Figure E9.36b, I've filled in the area outside of the line with more of the grass texture.

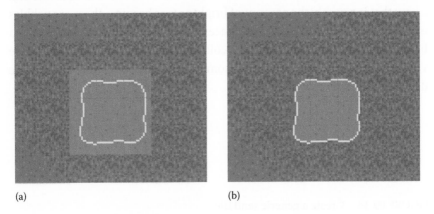

(a)   (b)

FIGURE E9.36   (a) We're creating 8 new transition tiles for a 9-slice. (b) Fill in appropriate area with grass.

Figure E9.36c (where we've colored the dividing line) and Figure E9.36d (which adds some cast shadow) show a poignant advantage of making a transition using the 9 slice method; it allows for proper light direction. We will explore another method of transition shortly that does not have this unique advantage.

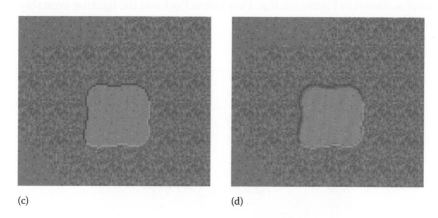

(c)

(d)

FIGURE E9.36 (c) We can color the line to imply lighting. (d) Add some cast shadow.

As we see in Figure E9.36, the 9 slice method allows you to build different sizes of sand without any trouble. This opens up a number of opportunities for laying out a scene but we still need four more tiles to really open up the more unique shapes.

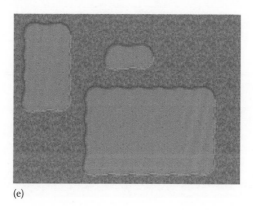

(e)

FIGURE E9.36 (e) The 9-slice can create various rectangles.

To build the new tiles, we'll create an area of sand surrounding a patch of grass creating a reverse 9 slice. To save effort, we can reuse the side and top tiles that we've already created. The bottom tile of the last 9 slice becomes the top tile of the new one, as you can see in Figure E9.36f. This is repeated for the other side and top tiles, so that we are only missing corners like what is shown in Figure E9.36g. This saves effort and the lighting even stays consistent.

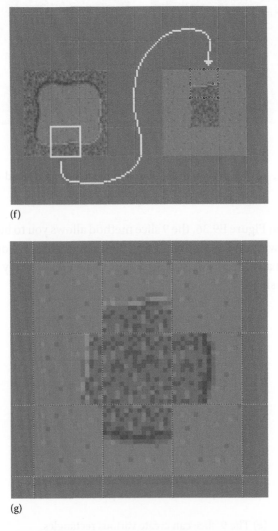

(f)

(g)

FIGURE E9.36 (f) Reuse tiles on opposite side for inversed 9-slice. (g) Inversed 9-slice needs corner tiles.

In Figure E9.36h, we'll outline the corner pieces, continuing to keep the light source consistent. Now we need only to complete the texture and add some shadow to have another finished 9 slice, as shown in Figure E9.36i.

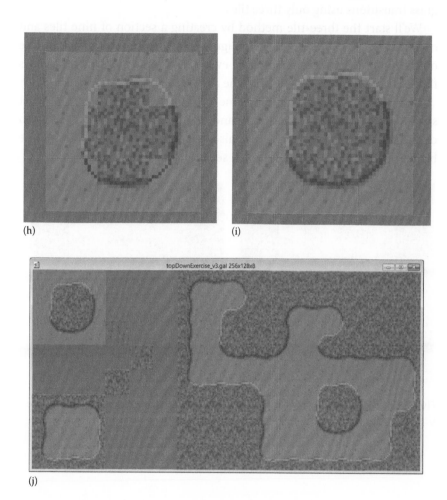

(h)

(i)

(j)

FIGURE E9.36   (h) Create corners with proper lighting. (i) Add cast shadow. (j) We are no longer confined to rectangles.

So we can see in Figure E9.36j that's we can put together these tiles in different ways to create unique shapes of sand and grass. In the end, we've actually needed 12 transition tiles to get the full range of shapes shown here.

This is a very common method, but not my personal favorite. The 9 slice method is great, but does necessitate a certain anal retentiveness about light direction. The final outcome can be very lovely, especially if you take lots of time to really flesh out each tile (which I did not). The issue is that I want to be far more lazy than the 9 slice method allows. Instead, let us rebuild these grass transitions using only three tiles.

We'll start the three-tile method by creating a section of nine tiles and outlining only two tiles as shown in Figure E9.37. It's important that the line on the top tile divides it in half fairly evenly. This is so that when the tile is flipped, it still aligns properly with the corner tile.

In Figure E9.38, I've colored the line a dark green and given it some cast shadow, and then in Figures E9.39 and E9.40 the grass texture has been duplicated to fill in the space. I will also add a bit of detail including some blades of grass in the sand that you'll see in the following images.

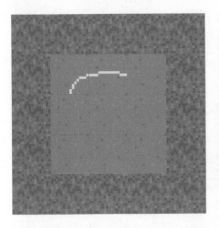

FIGURE E9.37   I'm too lazy for the 9-slice method.

FIGURE E9.38   We're going to ignore light direction.

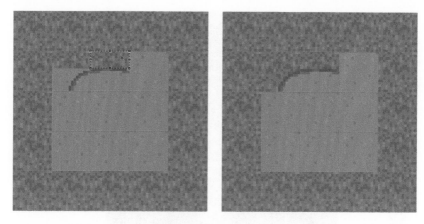

FIGURE E9.39   Fill in areas with grass.   FIGURE E9.40   Use two tiles instead of eight.

Now we need only to duplicate and flip those two tiles as shown in Figure E9.41 and we have the fully formed transition displayed in Figure E9.42.

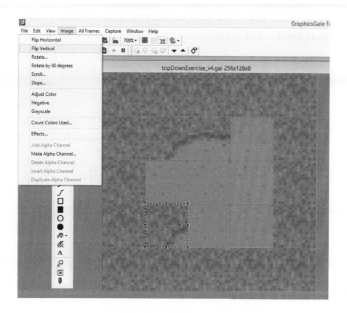

FIGURE E9.41   Duplicate and flip your tiles.

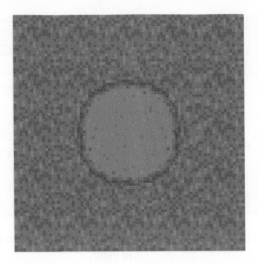

FIGURE E9.42   Two tiles create the impression of eight.

So with the two additional tiles built, we see in Figure E9.43 that we can easily build beds of sand of different sizes. We still need to create one more tile in order to build the more unique shapes, and we'll do it the same way the 9 slice was built... but faster.

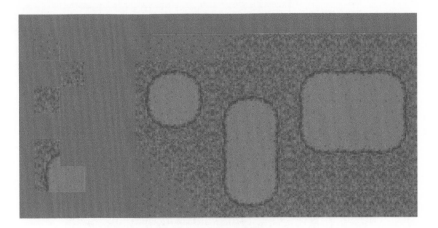

FIGURE E9.43   Our two tiles emulate the 9-slice.

In Figures E9.44 and E9.45, we've set things up just like we did when creating the inverse 9 slice. In this instance, however, we can reuse the same tile for all four sides.

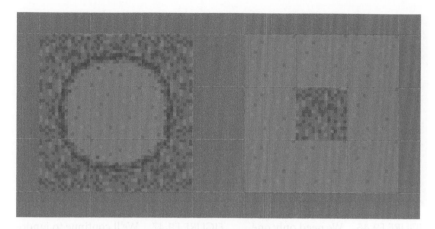

FIGURE E9.44   We still need an inverse transition.

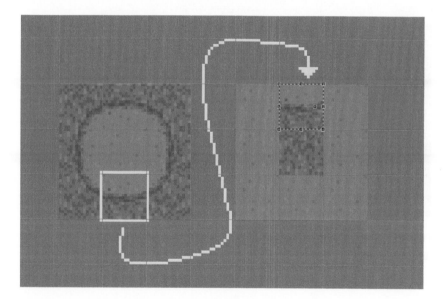

FIGURE E9.45   Once again we reuse the sides.

Nice, eh? Then we simply draw in the corner tile as shown in Figures E9.46 through E9.49. And Figure E9.50 shows how we can now use these tiles to make a number of unusual shapes.

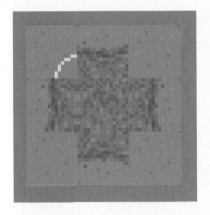

FIGURE E9.46   We need only one more tile.

FIGURE E9.47   We'll continue to ignore light direction.

FIGURE E9.48   Create some texture and cast shadow.

FIGURE E9.49   Violà!

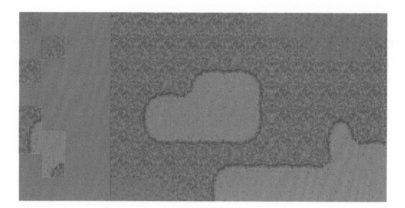

FIGURE E9.50   The three-tile method in action.

The three-tile method is a similar process to the 9 slice method, but significantly shorter. The shortcoming is that you cannot keep a genuine light direction throughout your scene when building this way. The advantages of this way over the 9 slice method are that it is faster to create the tiles, easier to build a scene with the tiles, and less chance of inconsistencies. It also means that your file sizes have the potential to be even smaller (which leads to faster compile times, download times for players, file management, etc.). You could also use the tile savings to create a load of variations to the edge, which helps to conceal the appearance of the grid within the scene.

Step 7: Variation Elation for the Game's Duration

Now let's really hammer on this topic of variation and build a number of variant tiles for the grass and sand. We've already built two types of grass that begins to give a bit of variation, but I like flower tiles. They're pretty. So to begin with, let's create some flowers to be added to the grass and I'll try to break them down to show how I make them.

In Figure E9.51a, I've illustrated the steps I use to build the flowers. Starting with one of the base grass textures, I'll add a few light green pixels as a flower stem or leaf and one of the brighter colors for the flower pedals. This is how each of the tiles is begun on the left-hand side. Next, I'll start to add some shadow being cast by the flower onto ground. Sometimes I'll give a bit of an outline to the flower so that it'll pop out a bit more, as I've done with the sunflower. Finally, I'll add some detail into the image in the form of texture and additional light gradient when applicable.

One last bit, to get the most out of our efforts, is to duplicate the final image with another color. This effectively gets two different variations while only expending the effort of building one.

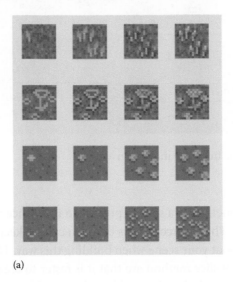

(a)

FIGURE E9.51   (a) Creating 4 new variation tiles.

I want to build another flower (well, two if we count the color shifted duplicate), but I want this one to be growing in a patch that's a bit wilder. To give the impression of a thicker/wilder grass, we'll want to use a higher contrast in the colors between dark and light.

I want to extend as little effort as possible so I'm going to build darker version of our current grass before building the high-contrast flower. I know that we're going to need a grass tile with some cast shadow later, so we'll preempt that effort now before building the flower.

You can see in Figure E9.15b that the tile is identical, but with all of the green colors shifted one value darker. You could potentially build a new grass tile with darker colors and ultimately that would likely be a more varied (and likely more desirable) aesthetic. But this way is much faster and in my experience does not detract from the scene in any noticeable way.

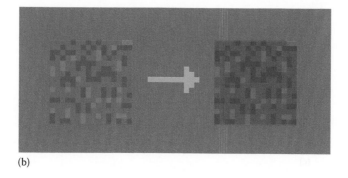

(b)

FIGURE E9.51   (b) Use a palette shift to create a darker grass tile.

There are a couple ways to create this tile that only take a couple moments. Many pixel art programs have a "darken" mode of some sort that will automatically shift the colors down in value by one slot. The problem with that is that it can sometimes give undesirable results (sometimes shifting the colors too dark or loosing colors that are close in value). The best practice is to have another file open with a different palette—a palette that is almost identical but with the colors shifted in position. Then when the tile is cut and paste into the file, it will read with the new colors. The steps involved in moving that tile back into your tile set can get a bit convoluted and they are rather program-specific, so I'll let you find your inner pixel genius work out those minute steps.

Now where were we? Oh yes, creating a wild flower. In Figure E9.51c, I've shown the steps to building the wild flower. First add three pixels of a light green to make some larger blades of grass, then add some dark green next to them to make them "pop" out a bit. You could potentially use this tile as another grass variation, but it would need to be altered quite a bit so that it wouldn't look so patterned when repeated. You can fix it up if you like, but I've got too many other nuggets of information I need to pass on to get sidetracked on this grass tile. I just added the pink flowers into the grass and placed some dark green next to them the same way I did with the blades of grass, but with a darker green so that they'd be more pronounced. Lastly, I added a yellow variation version to capitalize on my effort.

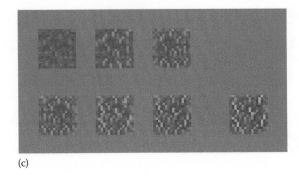

(c)

FIGURE E9.51   (c) Two new variation tiles, with a palette shift to create a third.

In Figure E9.52, we've used the tiles on the left to create the scene on the right and it's already starting to come together. Doesn't that look like a fantastic place to slay dragons?

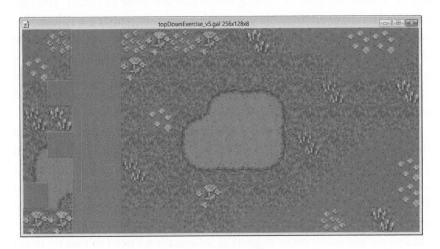

FIGURE E9.52   Just 12 tiles can create whole scenes.

In Figures E9.53 and E9.54, I've created some stones for the grass in a fairly standard way. I've begun with ugly grey blobs placed within the tile. You may notice that these are built with three stones, and that is no accident. I almost always use odd numbers when creating organic scenery, as even numbers tend to be read into patterns more easily by the human eye. Odd numbers of items are also frequently used in fine art and are sometimes cited as being aesthetically preferable.

Next, I've created light and dark in the grass, followed by some light and dark in the stone. Lastly, I've added some texture in the rock to make them look nifty.

I'm sure you've noticed that Figure E9.54 features an image built onto two consecutive tiles. I hope I didn't just blow your mind with that one. It turns out that we're allowed to do that! If you were to split the two halves apart they would look dreadful. But so long as they are together, they can add nice little dollops of augmented detail for a scene.

FIGURE E9.53   Using an odd number of rocks.

FIGURE E9.54   Using a two tile sequence.

Stones can be used for creating paths in your game, which are great for leading the player through your game environment.

Now that we've added so many variation tiles to the grass, the sand is getting a bit jealous. Let's add a couple of variation tiles there as well, to pretend that we love the sand as much as we love the grass. In Figure E9.55, you'll find some cacti being created in a method that should be starting to be kind of familiar: make blobs of color, add some light and shadow, make some variation to imply texture, and add a few pixel of cast shadow. This should be starting to feel somewhat standard by this point in your training.

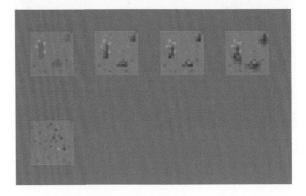

FIGURE E9.55   A couple of sand variation tiles.

Step 8: Rocking Out

My editor is telling me that she's about to fall asleep, so let's create something a bit trickier now. We're going to try to create a rock face. I think you can handle it.

We're going to start by making an outline of the texture. I think of building this similar to the shape of scales on a fish. If we take a look at Figure E9.56a we start by just making a couple of curves like the first image on the left. When we add the third curve in the second image, we do something sneaky by "wrapping" it around to the left side. That will significantly hide the edge of the tile. Then we continue to add arches, making sure that the lines at the top align with lines starting the curve at the bottom so that it repeats continuously without interruption like in Figure E9.56b.

(a)

FIGURE E9.56   (a) Creating a rock tile that repeats.

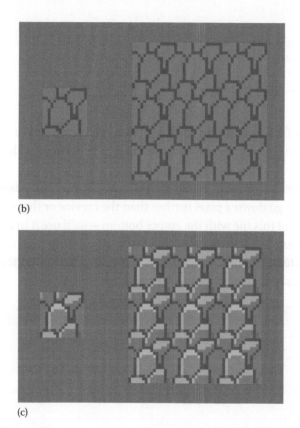

(b)

(c)

FIGURE E9.56   (b) Test the tiling. (c) Add highlights.

In Figure E9.56c, we've added a light grey to the top of the stones so to give the impression of a third dimension to this pattern.

In Figure E9.56d, we finish this tile by adding texture. We've added a bit of variation of grey within the dark and the light areas and added some green into the crevices to give the impression of moss. There's also been some brown added to imply some random splotches of dirt.

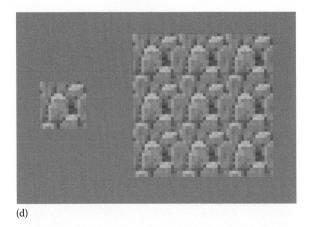

(d)

FIGURE E9.56   (d) Add texture.

This rock face looks pretty good, but we see in Figure E9.57a that the area where it connects with grass is a fairly harsh line that should be integrated together.

To resolve this, we start by stripping away the bottom. Notice that the rocks in front go down a pixel further than the crevice or the rocks in back. Make a copy of this tile with the empty bottom—we'll use it in a moment to create another tile. Then in the duplicate tile, we fill in the area at the bottom with a grass texture. I made it a bit dark at the edge, and gave the impression of some grass blades overlapping the rock.

(a)

FIGURE E9.57   (a) Creating a blend tile.

In Figure E9.57b, we can notice a similar problem where the top of the rock wall connects with the grass: it appears too angular and does not look at all appealing. This time we can use the tile that had been edited before to delete the top half of the stone tile, leaving behind the bottom half. Then we can add that to the grass tile creating a top edge to the wall as shown in Figure E9.57c.

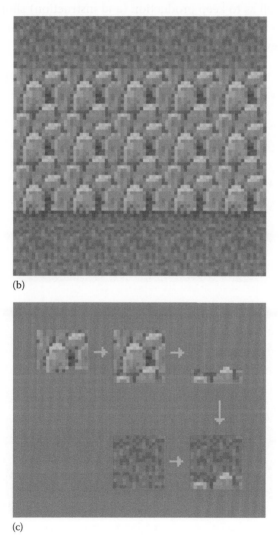

(b)

(c)

FIGURE E9.57   (b) A blend tile is needed for the top of the stone wall.
(c) Creating the other blend tile.

When the top edge is added to the wall in Figure E9.57d, the reappearance of the tall rock with the light color lends itself to a patterned appearance. For that reason I've decided to make the top of the rock a bit more even and added some dark to the grass to make the rock stand out.

Figure E9.57e shows that we're going to make an edge that works for both sides of the rock, despite the fact that it creates a slightly impossible lighting situation. Once again, I'm making this choice as an informed decision to save tiles as well as to keep production (and instruction) simple. Basically this tile has to be repeatable on the top and bottom, but connect up to the rock face believably on one side.

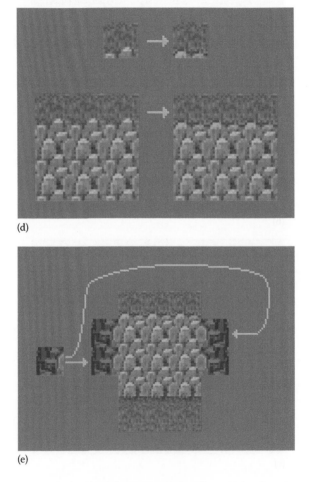

(d)

(e)

FIGURE E9.57   (d) Minimizing the patterned look. (e) An edge tile flipped to work on both sides.

In Figure E9.57f, we've made a couple more tiles that blend the top and bottom corners of the rock with the grass. And in Figure E9.57g we've added three more tiles to create the edges of the upper portion of the raised grass area.

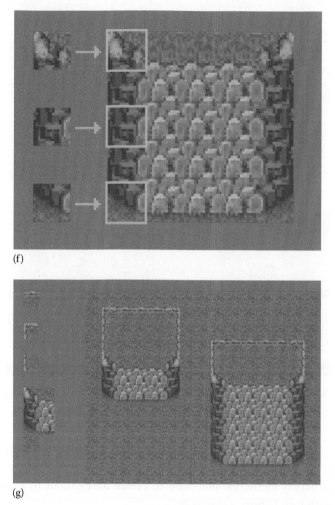

(f)

(g)

FIGURE E9.57   (f) Adding a top and bottom to the sides. (g) Three more tiles added for the top.

I'd like to add some cast shadow to give this addition have more presence. We have actually already built the main tile of darkened grass when creating our wild flowers (Figure E9.51b), so after placing it in the scene, we only need one more to blend the light with the shadow. After adding in the darker toned grass, we see in Figure E9.57h where things don't really match up. The edge at the back can be angular because it somewhat mirrors the shape of the structure, but we'll use a tile to blend the area in the front (Figure E9.57i).

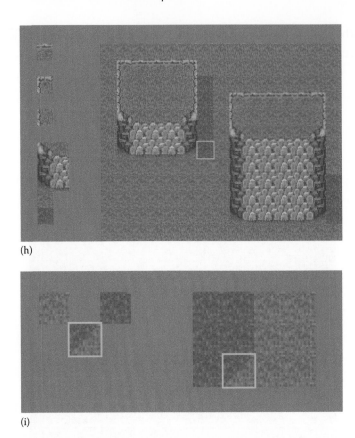

(h)

(i)

FIGURE E9.57   (h) Adding some cast shadow. (i) A blend tile for the cast shadow.

We're almost done building this structure, but I really want to take advantage of the grassy area on top of the rock. This seems like a nice place to add gameplay elements, but need to create an element to connect the bottom with top; I chose a stairway.

The main tile to build the stairway shown in Figure E9.57j uses a pattern with two dark pixels to imply the vertical part of a step followed by 3 pixels of light to imply the horizontal part of the step... But if you look carefully, you'll notice that it doesn't come out evenly and that we had to use an extra band of light pixels at the bottom. Bummer.

In Figure E9.57k, we've added a top and bottom tile with a nonexistent lighting source and can see the results. They look pretty good, but there is a significant improvement when we build in the light and dark sides as in Figure E9.57l, which brings tile count up to five for the steps.

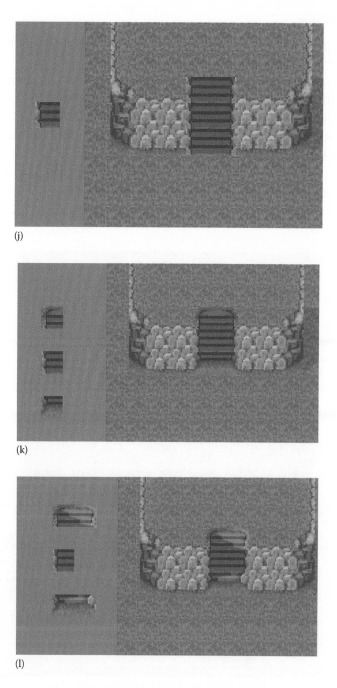

(j)

(k)

(l)

FIGURE E9.57   (j) A single tile flipped to create stairs. (k) Tiles for the top and bottom of the stairs. (l) Optional tiles to imply light direction.

Step 9: Water

So far so good, so let's add some water. In Figure E9.58, we have a repeating tile on the left and two variation tiles on the right.

Water usually has some sand or earth on the edge before becoming grassy, so we will do exactly that. We are going to use the three-tile method as we did with the sand to integrate it with the grass. In fact, we'll use the three tiles from the sand as guidelines for the edge of the water as shown in Figure E9.59a.

In Figures E9.59b through d we're pushing the sand back to make room for the water, which should come up to the middle of the tile. After creating a bit of shading to the tile and adding them to the scene, it looks like Figure E9.59.

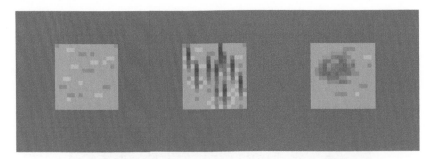

FIGURE E9.58   Water and variation tiles.

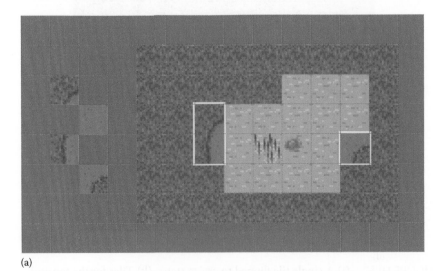

(a)

FIGURE E9.59   (a) Using sand as guidelines for water edges.

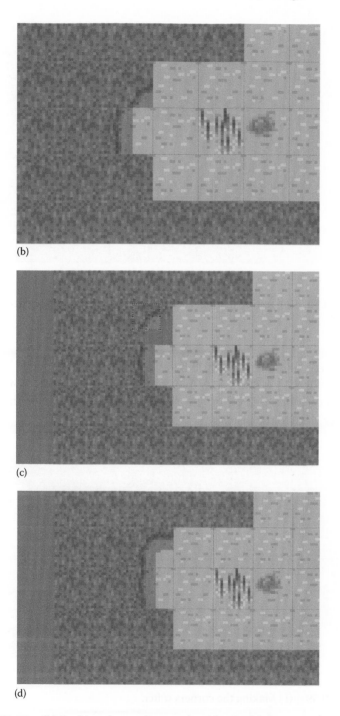

FIGURE E9.59   (b) Backing the sand up on the side tile. (c) Scooting the sand back on the corner tile. (d) Filling in the blank area with water.

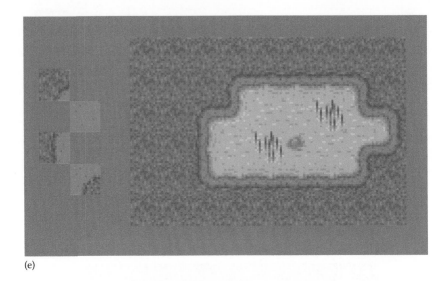

(e)

FIGURE E9.59   (e) Testing them in action after some shadow was added.

The edges still look a bit too angular for my taste, so in Figure E9.59f we make the angle a bit less severe. Also notice that we've given the water a bit of angled direction that echoes the shape of the land and made the water a bit darker close to the beach.

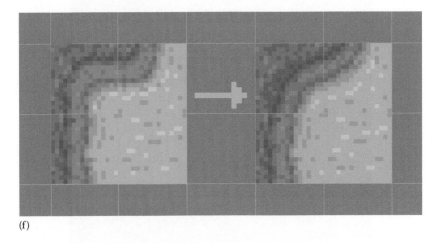

(f)

FIGURE E9.59   (f) Making the corners softer.

Step 10: Put It All Together

Ideally you've been putting together some environment ideas all the time while we've been creating the individual tiles, so this isn't really a step so much as some thoughts on how to use a tile set in interesting ways.

Over the course of this exercise we've created grass, sand, and water as well as some variant tiles and it's time to start using these to put together scenes in your game. Figures E9.60 through E9.62 show some different ways that you can configure these tiles within a game setting.

One thing to note is that you can definitely use your tile set to create gameplay. Looking at Figure E9.60, you can see that the arrangement of stones and flowers within the grass create a clear path that the player can easily follow.

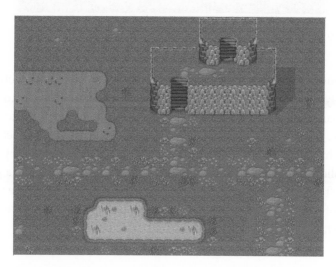

FIGURE E9.60   Use flowers or stones (or both!) to create paths.

We can also use the elements of the environment to suggest other ideas, which can result in some very satisfying puzzle elements. You can use the shape or configuration of the tiles to create a secondary image, as in Figure E9.61 where the lake has been put together to resemble a key.

FIGURE E9.61   Create unique scenes while reusing assets.

Of course, these elements can also be configured in more subtle ways that imply nuance only to the more observant player. In Figure E9.62, there is a primary path that leads upward toward a patch of sand at the top of the structure. But there is also a more subtle path that veers to the left at the bottom that is created from the second type of grass and some stray stones. If you follow that path, it leads to an area where the flowers make a pattern on the left side of the stone structure. This would be a perfect place to build a secret of some sort into your game, as there is some degree of direction to the player, but likely to be missed without close observation.

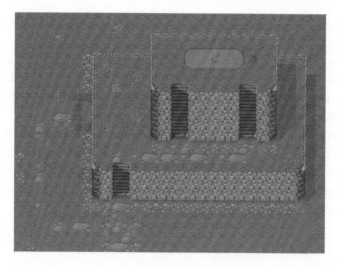

FIGURE E9.62   Use accent tiles to create subtle clues.

We could continue to grow our tile set, adding more sorts of terrain to our sand, grass, and water—adding interior spaces, caves, etc.—but here is where we will move on to something different. That being said, if you plan to use what you've created for your game—I encourage you to continue expanding on this foundation to really add a high degree of variety and variation.

By this juncture you should have a good handle on how to create these kind of tiles and our joined effort is better spent moving in a different direction and getting exposure to some other ideas.

EXERCISE 9.2: CREATING A SIMPLE SIDE-VIEW TILE SET

In our last exercise we used 16 × 16 tiles to create tiles to build a game from a top-down perspective, but this time we are going to change things to use some of the concepts we've talked about in different ways.

For this exercise we are going to use 32 × 32 tiles to build a side-scrolling sort of environment.

To begin with, create a new file with a canvas size of 640 × 480 and an 8-bit palette. This will give us a canvas to work with that is 20 tiles wide and 15 tiles high.

With this sort of environment we are going to work from back to front. That is to say that we will first create the things that appear farthest away and create the closest objects last. This will make it easy to visualize what we are doing in context and also help us to see the results of our effort in real time.

First we are going to create a gradient like what is seen in Figure E9.63 and use it to build the sky. If you take a moment to look at this gradient, you may (or may not) notice that it looks a bit different than the gradients we've built so far and I want to take a moment to explain why.

This gradient changes in more than just value. It does change value going from darker on the left to lighter on the right, but it also shifts its hue as well: the colors blend from purple on the left to blue in the middle and right. The saturation also changes through the gradient—being more intense in the center colors.

FIGURE E9.63   A 5 color sky gradient.

With that built, we can use those colors to create bands of color in the sky like Figure E9.64. Notice that the bands of color get smaller and smaller as they get toward the top of the screen; this gives a subtle impression of atmosphere and usually reads better than a perfectly even ramp. For this reason, I haven't gotten to worry about where these bands fall in relation to the grid (yet).

FIGURE E9.64   A simple sky background.

One behavior of color ramps that is particularly useful for building sky is that the tighter the gradient, the more they will blend together, as demonstrated in Figure E9.65. But for now we will leave these colors as they are on the right-hand side because we are going to use dithering to blend these guys together in just a moment.

FIGURE E9.65   Gradients with low contrast blur better.

Although we filled in the whole canvas with sky, we can actually think of this as one vertical strip like the left side of Figure E9.66 repeated over and over again. Although the whole bottom side is really the same tile, we can actually focus all of our effort just on the tiles on top half.

So now we will use a dither to create the impression that the colors are blending from one to the next. This is done exactly as the first sort of dither shown in Section 9.5. The only major difference is that this is being done with 32 × 32 tiles instead of 16 × 16, so it will take roughly four time longer to complete the process. When you're done it should look something similar to the strip on the right-hand side of Figure E9.67.

FIGURE E9.66   A vertical slice of the sky background.

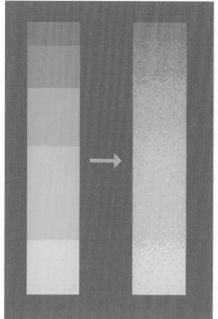

FIGURE E9.67   Using anti-aliasing for additional blending.

FIGURE E9.68   Using some texture for the primary sky tile.

I've decided to add a bit of pattern shown in Figure E9.68 into the last tile that covers the bottom half of the picture. This is not necessary and basically falls into the category of "effort spent on things no one will ever notice," but still I like the result.

Now we'll create a new layer in GraphicsGale. Just go to the Layers window (Figure E9.69) and click on the little button shaped like a downward arrow pointing toward a line on the left-hand side. Then select the "Add…" option as shown in Figure E9.70.

FIGURE E9.69   The layers window in GraphicsGale.

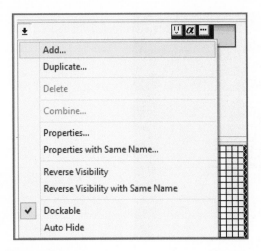

FIGURE E9.70   Add a new layer.

Now let's add some mountains. We're going to block them out as rectangular tiles as seen in Figure E9.71 but don't worry, we'll give them a proper profile shape very shortly. We've done this using the second lightest sky color that will make them appear to sit back because of atmospheric perspective (that we talked about in Section 7.4).

FIGURE E9.71   Roughing out some mountains.

Now we will add a proper profile shape to the mountains. (I told you we would be doing this shortly!) I've drawn three tiles shown in Figure E9.72 that we'll use to make our blue squares look more like a mountain range.

You can see the dramatic change in Figure E9.73 and see how it looks in our scene in Figure E9.74.

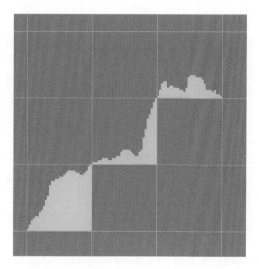

FIGURE E9.72   Edges for the mountains.

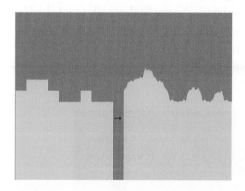

FIGURE E9.73   Adding the edges to the mountains.

FIGURE E9.74   Mountains in the distance.

Now you have a small decision to make in your future: do you want that mountain range to scroll, or do you want it to be static in the background. It is nice to have your background in multiple layers so that they can scroll at different speeds (called parallax) that gives a lovely illusion of depth. In many cases your programmer may impose a hard limit on the amount of parallax layers, and since the mountains sit so far back it is a good candidate for merging into the sky layer. It's your decision (or perhaps it may be your programmer's choice).

Now to get more mileage out of our mountains we're going to reuse those tiles by simply duplicating them and making them two shades darker (Figure E9.75).

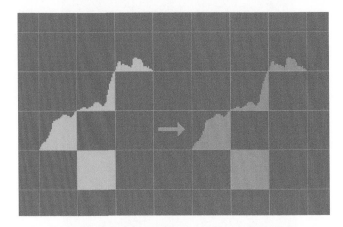

FIGURE E9.75   Reusing the tiles for a closer mountain range.

But because these mountains are going to be a bit closer to the viewer, we're going to give them a little bit of detail. We made these tiles two shades darker so we can use the in-between color to add some highlight to the peaks of the mountain, as shown in Figure E9.76. Then we can add these mountains onto a new layer and we can see how the added texture subtly improves the image in Figure E9.77.

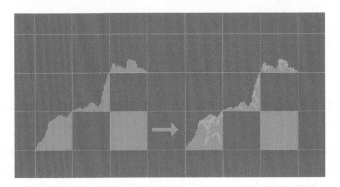

FIGURE E9.76   Adding highlights.

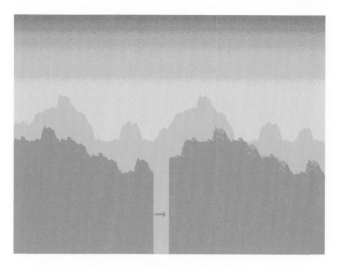

FIGURE E9.77   Before and after adding the highlights.

At this point the tops of the newer mountains have a little bit of depth, but that also makes the lower part that is entirely one color read as being very flat. Once again we are going to reuse our tiles to add some detail with minimal effort.

In Figure E9.78, we are taking a duplicate of the tiles that create the profile of the mountains and add them right on top of the blue creating the nonprofile parts, creating texture that can be used in the body of the mountain shown in the right side of the picture. At the end of this process we should have something fairly spiffy, like the background shown in Figure E9.79.

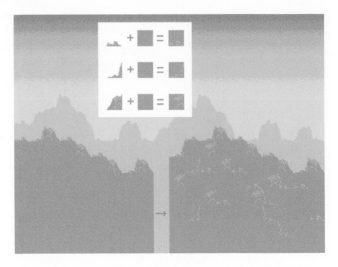

FIGURE E9.78   Adding additional highlight textures.

FIGURE E9.79   Light colors used for atmospheric perspective.

I'm sure that you've noticed that we've only used light colors so far to imply atmospheric perspective in our scene. That's one of the things I like about you—you're observant.

We are actually going to grow this tile set for two types of environments: an outdoor scene as well as a cityscape. This will give our environment a great deal of versatility in terms of its use. For the most part they will be used separately but there may also be cases where we can "mix and match" them together, so that occasionally our tiles will actually do double duty.

We're going to start with the outdoor scene, to continue the theme of organic matter, starting with some foliage off in the distance and grass bridging the distance between the background and foreground.

First I want to build some trees in the distance, but we're going to need a few more colors to make that happen. Figure E9.80 shows the three colors that I've added to the palette. The new colors are a light blue–green, so that they won't conflict with the higher intensity and contrast colors we will be using for the foreground later. This will help these background trees to appear to sit back and create the horizon. For this tile, I've actually only used the two lighter colors.

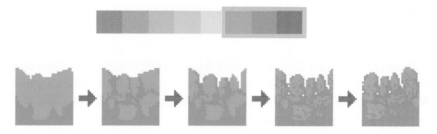

FIGURE E9.80   Adding 3 colors to create some distant bushes.

One thing I'd like to point out is that the final tile shown on the right side of Figure E9.80 is almost identical to the tile adjacent to it. The only difference is that I've shifted its position horizontally to the left on the tile so that the tree on the edge isn't split in half between the two tiles. This will make it easier to create a variation tile.

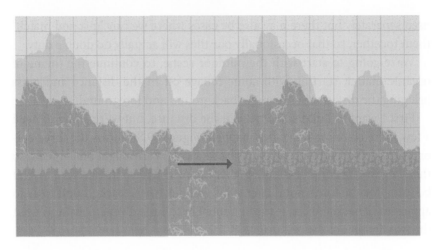

FIGURE E9.81   One tile makes a big change in the scene.

Figure E9.81 shows how we started by a simply setting a horizon and then added detail within that one tile from Figure E9.80. Notice also that the darker green goes all the way to the bottom of the screen; this will help the parallax to be a bit smoother.

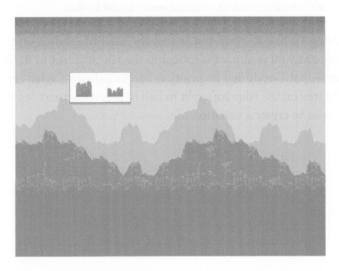

FIGURE E9.82   Adding a variation tile.

In Figure E9.82, we've added a variation tile to the horizon, allowing the tree line to appear a bit more varied.

Now we'll add another layer to our scene and add a couple more trees, shown in Figure E9.83. I've started with a rather sloppy outline and filled it in with the most neutral tone. Then I blocked out the areas of dark and added in some areas of light and cleaned up the lines in the image.

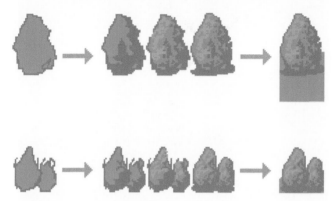

FIGURE E9.83   From sloppy to clean.

In the final images on the right, I've added the color of the ground to adequately cover the background tiles when the background is in parallax. That is to say that once in game, this layer may not be static and will move in relation to the other layers. A simple grass is needed to tile at the bottom (which could be a single color) to make sure that the layers scroll without hovering in the air. Figure E9.84 shows the layer in isolation and in context to show how the orientation of the background can change.

FIGURE E9.84   Fill in the bottom to avoid parallax issues.

The less-than-desirable outcome of not including the grass at the bottom is shown in Figure E9.85. Ugh.

FIGURE E9.85   An example of a parallax issues.

At this juncture I want to create some tiles on our interactive layer—which will constitute of the objects that the character can have contact with. In the environment this could consist of solid ground, platforms, walls, or anything else that the character would collide with. In homage to the 8-bit gaming trope of the platformer, let's begin with a platform.

Once again, we'll want to add some new colors to our palette. The new colors should be higher in saturation (intensity) to make the interactive tiles stand out clearly from the background. The new colors should also have a higher contrast of value, so you may need more colors in your ramp to pull it off nicely. Figure E9.86 displays my current palette, with the new colors on the bottom. I've used another gradient of green and some browns that I'll need to build my platforms.

FIGURE E9.86   Saturated colors added for the interactive layer.

Figure E9.87 demonstrates the steps I take to build a platform. An important factor in the building process is that in most games the collision detection is built as a rectangular bounding box. That is to say that the places that are solid—that the character collides with—are usually rectangular. As a general rule I build my tiles right out to the edge of the tile (give one or two pixels) so that the behaviors the player will experience will make sense visually.

To begin with, I simply block out the areas where the grass and dirt are going to be with solid colors. Then I add the dark to the side of the grass, defining the walking area on top, followed by some cast shadow on the dirt area.

All while I'm making changes, I keep duplicating the left tile and flipping it to create the tile on the right so that the platform is made by one tile mirrored to create the other side. Reusing the tile has more to do with the ease of using tiles to create a scene later in the process than aesthetic preference, and whether you follow this practice is genuinely up to you.

Next (on the top right) I add some midtone to the grass, followed by a bit of outline on both the grass and dirt. Lastly, I add some texture detail to the grass and the earth resulting in a nice little platform. In truth, I tend to build these with the background visible on lower layers as shown in Figure E9.88. That way I can make adjustment as needed so that the colors and size work nicely within the context that they will be used.

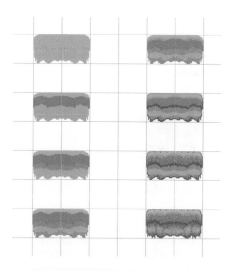

FIGURE E9.87   Creating a platform tile (mirrored).

FIGURE E9.88   I frequently build over a background layer.

That's a pretty nice platform, especially considering that it consists of only one tile. Now we'll build a second tile that will allow this platform to be extended. Figure E9.89 shows that I've begun by duplicating the tile on the right and placing it in the center. Then I've taken a vertical strip from one part of the tile (shown in red) and duplicated it to cover up the edge. Violà! We now have an extendable platform built lickety-split.

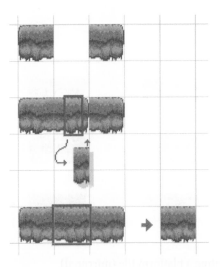

FIGURE E9.89   Reusing part of the existing tile to create a middle tile.

In Figure E9.90, we see the result of our effort and it works within the context quite well. One thing that there is something that disturbs be a bit though—our platforms appear to be simply hanging in midair. Many platform games do fine just like this—certainly many of the most famous platform games of all time use this floating platform method and we can probably get away with it too.

FIGURE E9.90   Two tiles can create different sized platforms.

But because it bugs me, we're going to look into one way of resolving this visual incongruence. You'll need to add another layer to the scene in between the platforms and the rest of the background. We'll also add a couple more colors that are a blend between the brown of the platform and the blue–green of the grass, like the last three on the right-hand side of Figure E9.91. I've added three colors, but we may only need the two lighter colors.

FIGURE E9.91   Three more colors added.

This is an instance where we're going to deviate from the traditional method of building tiles, although you could do this tile by tile if you choose.

Basically the game plan is to draw in an organic stone/clay structure to support the platforms so that they don't look like they're hanging in midair. I don't believe there is much time to be saved by building this part tile by tile, so I'm going to revert to a freehand technique.

First I'm going to simply rough in the general shape I want to support the platforms, as shown in Figure E9.92.

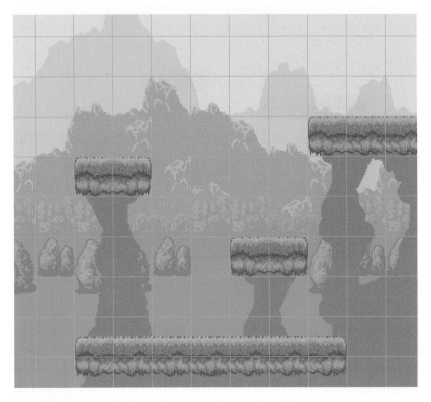

FIGURE E9.92   Roughing out a context for the platforms.

Although this was started freehand, I've still kept the general shapes within as few tiles as possible. I began with the vertical part on the left, and then decided to duplicate that shape and reuse it a couple times (flipped on the x-axis in one instance).

Next I want those platforms to cast a bit of shadow, so I'm going to mask the color and draw the shadow in only on that shade of brown. Masking is super useful for working on a single color at a time without disturbing any of the others. Simply click on the mask button and then click on the color you want to mask around. That's it—Now we can start drawing in shadow where you want it to go, as shown in Figure E9.93.

FIGURE E9.93   Adding shadow.

To blend the shadow, I'm going to use a patterned dither. This will serve the dual purposes of making the edge of the cast shadow softer, while simultaneously giving the surface more texture. Starting with the left, the altered image looks like Figure E9.94.

In Figure E9.95, we duplicate the image to reuse it a couple of times and continue this look into the rest of the image. I've also tried to reuse tiles whenever it is feasible.

After that I took the shapes used to make the mountains in the background to build some more tiles that are more reusable, as shown in Figure E9.96. I guess I just couldn't help building them into tiles. Figure E9.97 shows how we integrate everything into the background image.

FIGURE E9.94   Using dithering to add detail.

FIGURE E9.95   Reuse the shape when possible.

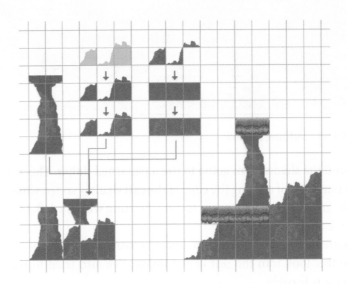

FIGURE E9.96   Building texture tiles from existing tiles.

I really like this sort of image—where there is a common background element to unify the items that would otherwise be floating in air. Unfortunately there are some serious drawbacks to arranging your level this way. Beyond the more limited amount of reuse available, this sort of thing can easily set you up for trouble down the road.

Developing games—and designing levels in particular—is an iterative process and this technique doesn't lend itself to lots of adjustment. Consider what happens when you decide your level needs to be more vertical and need to place everything in a completely different spot... All of your work would be lost (or at least in need of major readjustment).

This sort of thing really works best when your level is already complete and play-tested. It looks nice, but once again, you've been warned about a major potential pitfall.

FIGURE E9.97   Integrating the new tiles.

But whether you choose to put in this sort of environment uniting structure like Figure E9.97 or not, it's usually nice to have a bit of foliage to break up the area. In Figure E9.98, I've added a patch of grass and some bushes, using the same colors as the rocky structure.

FIGURE E9.98   Adding foliage to break up the area.

One thing that I would like to draw your attention to while we've got these as an example is the profile of the layer. When an environment has multiple scrolling layers, I've found that creating a unique silhouette for the shape of the objects makes the layer very aesthetically appealing.

If we take a look at the shape of the layers that would be scrolling in silhouette, we can see there is a dramatic difference depending on the details we give. If we take a look at Figures E9.99 and E9.100 we see that the silhouetted layer is rather dull and lifeless. This sort of shape is like a cubical-bound office worker that has become resigned to the position and has lost the drive to go out and find another angle on life.

Now let's compare that with Figures E9.101 and E9.102. Clearly the second images have a lot more going on and have more appeal in silhouette form. These are more like former office workers that have left their job to follow their passion of writing books about how to create video game graphics.

The rather curious thing is that in addition to looking nice, the more complicated silhouette the layer creates—the more it reads as being believable to the viewer.

FIGURE E9.99   The scene without detail tiles.

FIGURE E9.100   Silhouette of scene without detail tiles.

FIGURE E9.101   The scene with detail tiles.

FIGURE E9.102   Silhouette of scene with detail tiles.

Let's also take a quick moment to consider what would happen if we used more muted colors in the foreground and higher intensity for the colors in the background. We would risk completely losing the sense of depth as seen in Figure E9.103. The viewer's eye want to go to the back area of the picture and does not want to focus on the background. Woof.

FIGURE E9.103 Don't fight atmospheric perspective.

If you've been following along, you should have the tiles to build a nice organic background. But what if you want to create something more urban? Let's expand our tile set to include some buildings, perhaps for a different level. When we're done, we should be able to create something like Figure E9.104 relatively easily.

FIGURE E9.104   A simple urban environment.

FIGURE E9.105   Adding colors to the palette.

But first things first—we're going to need more colors. Figure E9.105 shows that we've added a gray gradient to the top row of colors that will be used for buildings in the distance. We've also added a row of colors on the bottom that will give us colors we can use for the closer buildings.

That being said, we (perhaps ironically) will be reusing two of our colors used in the sky to create the most distant buildings as displayed in

Figure E9.106. These will be in the far background of the image, so we are using the palette to help these buildings appear to be farther from the viewer in the picture.

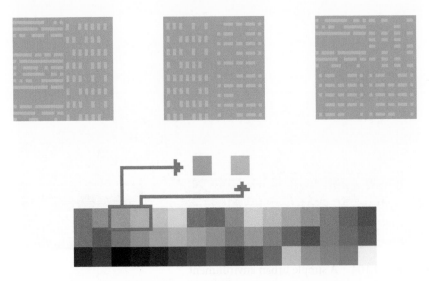

FIGURE E9.106   Using sky colors for buildings in the distance.

As you can see from the example, the buildings in the background can be almost comically simple. In this case, each tile is giving the impression of two buildings next to each other. This is only suggested by the arrangement of windows rather than by explicitly defining a boundary. This will help the buildings appear to blur into the background, helping the foreground to stand out clearly.

Left as it is (Figure E9.107), this would be too rough even for the background. So we'll make a handful of tiles (Figure E9.108) that define the distant city's skyline. I've decided to use a tile that only has a few pixels to create the impression of some items on the roof, improving the silhouette for the layer.

FIGURE E9.107   Roughing out a far background.

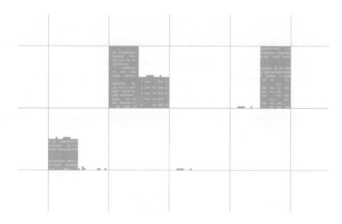

FIGURE E9.108   Tiles to create a better silhouette.

Once these new tiles are added into the scene like in Figure E9.109, the tiles read much more like buildings. As we add more buildings in the foreground with more contrast and detail, the viewer's eye will "read" these as buildings as much from the context as from the actual drawing.

FIGURE E9.109   Far background with the additional tiles.

Now we'll repeat the process with larger buildings and slightly darker colors to create some new tiles seen in Figure E9.110. In this case I've taken the darkest color from the sky and used it as the base color for the buildings and a gray as the window color. When added to a new layer in the scene as in Figure E9.111, the image starts to build the appearance of depth.

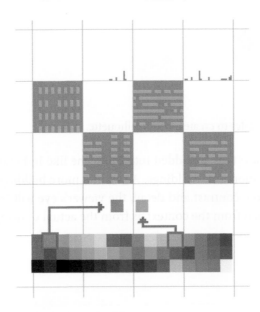

FIGURE E9.110   Creating closer buildings.

FIGURE E9.111   Roughing out the closer background.

The next layer we'll build another building, still larger and darker than the previous layers—shown in Figure E9.112. I've actually made the impression of things going on in the window although it is unlikely to be noticed by any players.

You may notice that I've used a dull green as the window shadow. It gives the color a bit of flavor and seems to work nicely. I'll also point out a grievance that I have in my own work: the top left tile is extremely wasteful. The whole tile is used for only a handful of pixels and this is definitely suboptimal. I've made this concession for the sake of creating a slightly more interesting profile shape but this is definitely a tradeoff situation.

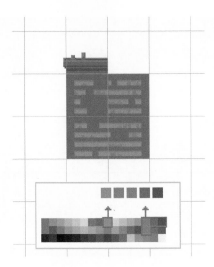

FIGURE E9.112   Building the third and closest background.

Finally, we can start into our main layer and we'll do it by beginning with the most common tile—a brick that tiles seamlessly. The first step in Figure E9.113 shows to start by creating the general brick pattern. The bricks in the pattern all have a uniform height—three pixels of red followed by one pixel of the dark color for the mortar.

The next step shows to add a lighter color to the top and left side to give the impression of depth to the pattern. The last step shows that I've added some variation to the mortar that gives the brick texture a more weathered appearance and adds some zing to an otherwise static pattern.

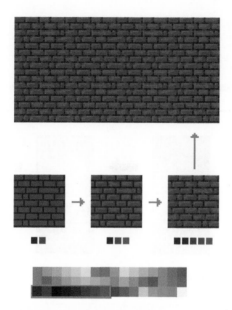

FIGURE E9.113   Making a repeating brick tile.

In Figure E9.114, we go through the steps of constructing a window that will go with the brick texture starting with only the barest impression of a frame and windowsill. Next we add some detail and the shadow cast from being slightly recessed from the frame. In this case we create the window shininess from diagonal lines of varying thickness. There are other ways to create the window shine aesthetic, but this method is fairly independent of the rest of the environment so we avoid contextual inconsistencies.

We then add the window to the brick tiles and add some cast shadow to integrate the window into the context.

Looking at Figure E9.115, we can see that the foreground is actually starting to shape up. Obviously this is not enough to look complete, but looks startlingly good considering that we've only created three tiles.

To complete the tiles for this building, we need to create some form of roof and something defining the edge for the building.

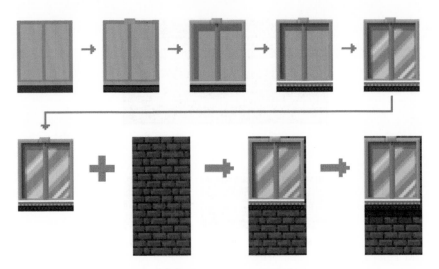

FIGURE E9.114   Creating a window.

FIGURE E9.115   Our cityscape so far.

In Figure E9.116, we create a roof ledge using one tile for the main section and an extra tile to create the left (and right) edge. We also create another brick tile to give the impression of cast shadow. In Figure E9.117, we build a pattern to be used on the edge of the building and add it to the brick.

I wasn't able to make that tile look good when flipped, so I built separate tile for each side of the building.

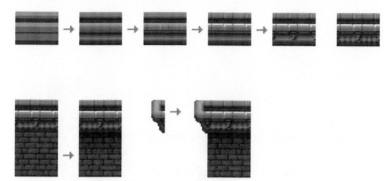

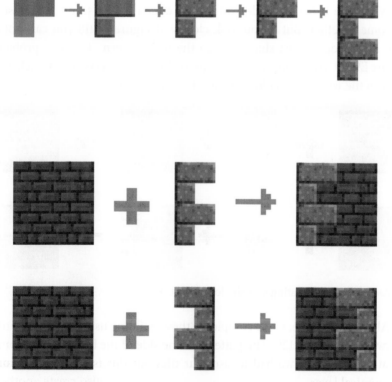

FIGURE E9.116   Adding a roof to the brick.

FIGURE E9.117   Adding accent tiles to the brick.

FIGURE E9.118   The accented edges need cast shadow.

When the ledge and side pattern are added to the scene, things start to come together. But if you look closely at Figure E9.118 you can notice that ledge doesn't cast shadow onto the wall pattern. This is a problem. Figure E9.119 goes through the steps of building a version of each wall pattern tile with cast shadow to complete the buildings.

FIGURE E9.119   Creating cast shadow accent tiles.

All said and done, we've completed these building using only the 10 tiles shown in Figure E9.120. The pattern on the side of the building was somewhat expensive, as we had to use four tiles but this is ultimately a fairly economical layer.

Now let's give these buildings a bit more vitality by creating some variation tiles. In Figure E9.121, I've created an alternative side pattern, some roof ledge variations, a moldy version of brick, and a window with a creepy guy looking out.

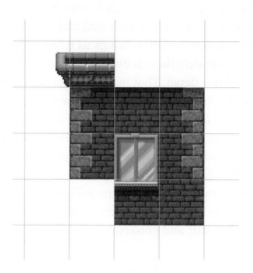

FIGURE E9.120   The tiles used in the main layer.

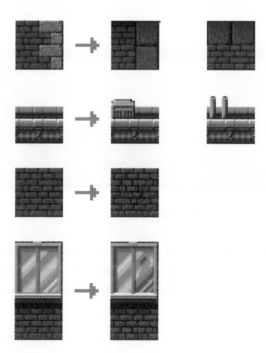

FIGURE E9.121   Adding variation tiles.

Once this is added to a dynamic situation (like a game) these variations aren't really noticed by the player at a conscious level but do affect the overall "feel." Cumulatively these can make the difference between a level that feels unique and interesting over one that feels dull and repetitive.

The creepy guy window variation brings us to an interesting point that I'd like to discuss. Ultimately there is almost no chance that anyone would perceive this level of fine detail. That makes this an incredible opportunity to slip an inside joke into your game. Perhaps it would amuse you to create a caricature of a friend or throw in a reference to an imaginary rock group. Just keep in mind that *with mild power comes mild responsibility*. In this litigious society I encourage you to respect copyright and avoid anything that would be totally offensive or inappropriate.

When we add these new tiles to our scene in Figure E9.122, things actually start to look fairly polished. If those layers parallax in the game, the effect will be even more dramatic and powerful.

FIGURE E9.122   The finished environment.

I imagine this environment as one where superheroes would be moving along the roof ledge, jumping from building to building. If I were to continue to build the tile set, I'd add things that protrude from the building that could act as additional platforms in the game. Air conditioning units could work as additional play surfaces, as well as scaffolding or fire escapes. I would try to work the platforms into the tiles as believable entities within the environment as much as possible.

We've spent so much time on constructing these buildings, let's not forget about the organic tiles we built earlier. Obviously we can build the two different types of environments separately, but we can also mix and match the tiles—but we have to be careful because things don't always match up smoothly.

Figure E9.123 shows one way in which we could screw up the scene by using the tiles incoherently. In truth, we could almost get away with this if the buildings were shown at ground level rather than being in the air. Figure E9.124 works a bit more reasonably and I'll bet that you could come up with something better still.

FIGURE E9.123   Layer priority gone awry.

FIGURE E9.124   Mixing up tiled environments.

All in all we've built this environment from the 80 tiles shown in Figure E9.125.

FIGURE E9.125   80 tiles create the whole tileset for this environment.

Let's wrap up this chapter by talking about managing your tiles. In most cases a game's level editor will organize the tiles something like what is shown in Figure E9.125—eliminating any unused tiles. This may be efficient for the computer but it isn't really the easiest to use for those of you that happen to be human.

That looks like a bit of a mess, but let's take a look at these tiles arranged in couple other ways. Figure E9.126 shows the same set organized from closest to the viewer on the left to farthest on the right. This can be useful, especially for fine tuning your palette (which I won't do today on account of extreme laziness).

But overall, I find it best to work with something like Figure E9.127 if possible. By keeping each tile type together and partially constructed it becomes very easy to find whatever you are looking for to build with. The tiles that have only a few pixels describing a bit of detail over a distant building can easily become totally obscure without context. This way everything stays clear in the mind's eye.

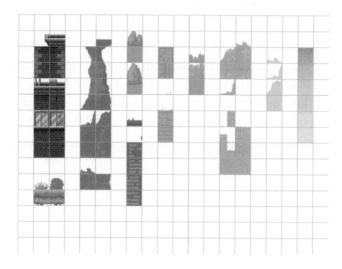

FIGURE E9.126   Tiles organized by layer priority.

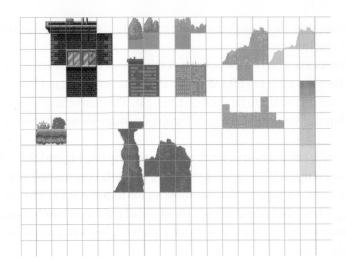

FIGURE E9.127   Tiles organized by type.

All in all we've built this environment from only 80 tiles. Put together this would be only one 320 × 256 image that uses less than 50 colors. But broken into pieces it can be used to create countless environments within your game. I don't believe that I can articulate just how efficient that is in terms of computer space management. Although I think I just did. Weird.

CHAPTER 10

You're Doing It Wrong

Things to Avoid

Aᶠᵗᵉʳ ˢᵖᵉⁿᵈⁱⁿᵍ ˢᵒ ᵐᵘᶜʰ ᵗⁱᵐᵉ ᵗᵃˡᵏⁱⁿᵍ about good ways to do things, I thought it fitting to write a chapter on what not to do. There are certain issues that seem to pop up and rear their ugly heads on a fairly common basis so it seems fitting to address them now—before your milestone is due.

10.1 BANDING AND "SUPER PIXELS"

Banding is a common mistake among novice Pixel Artists—even folks with some great art talent. The good news is that once you understand what to look for, it is often fairly easy to avoid (or at least substantially mitigate). I say mitigate rather than eliminate because there may be instances where it cannot be entirely abolished. As you work in smaller resolutions it becomes more and more difficult to completely avoid the banding effect.

Banding is an effect that occurs when sets of color or shape "end" in the same place, causing an imaginary line that bands the unrelated items together. One of the most common places that this occurs is when the shading on an object line up with the outline of the same item.

The most obvious example of banding is creating what is sometimes called a "super pixel". This is where multiple lines of shading all line up exactly when creating a diagonal line. The opportunity to imply a smoother line is lost, in effect giving no higher fidelity than a large pixel. Figure 10.1 shows a super pixel on the left with an example of how to resolve it on the right.

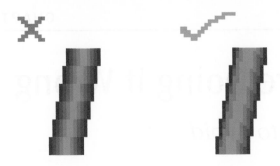

FIGURE 10.1   The dreaded "super pixel."

Perhaps the most heinous crime you can commit as a Pixel Artist is to create the dreaded super pixel. There is only one instance that this may be forgivable: if there is only one small segment that is being repeated in code to create a wire or vine that moves. Even this may be unforgivable.

Of course, some banding is less obvious to casual observation. Take the example in Figure 10.2 and we can see how the lazy gradients on the left can create some substantial banding. The corrected version on the right may still have some issues to resolve, but the banding has been dealt with.

FIGURE 10.2   Avoid banding when possible.

In Figure 10.3, the issue is even more subtle, but certainly still a situation that can be improved upon. Take a moment and look at the green blob on the left—can you find some banding? It doesn't leap out quite as much as the previous examples, so you may need to look closely.

FIGURE 10.3   Sometimes banding can be subtle.

Figure 10.4 explicitly shows the specific areas where the pixels line up by each of the eyes. The issue is subtle but once you become attuned to it, it becomes difficult *not* to see and a bit of a bane. Now you can look back at Figure 10.3 to see how I've resolved the offending spots without making changes that are terribly noticeable.

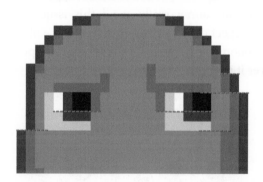

FIGURE 10.4   Subtle banding revealed.

10.2 TOO MUCH ANTI-ALIAS

If some anti-alias is good then more is better, right? Wrong. For the love all things good in the world, take it easy on the anti-aliasing! A little bit goes a long way. Too much and the picture will look blurry, making it look an awful lot like it was a larger picture reduced in size, losing image quality indiscriminately (Figure 10.5).

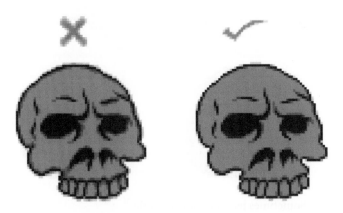

FIGURE 10.5   Avoid using too much anti-alias.

10.3 POOR LINE QUALITY

We talked about line quality earlier in the book but it has so much potential for mayhem that it must be iterated. Because a line is actually built of a bunch of squares it is super important to have it appear intentional.

Unfortunately, you cannot really avoid this issue by excluding lines because the same aspect comes up for the shape of the object you are creating (albeit less pronounced). I guess it should be called "poor shape quality" instead; whatever it is, try to avoid it.

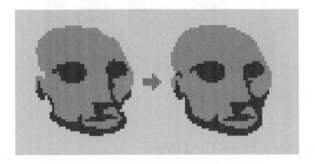

FIGURE 10.6   Even shapes have edge quality.

Figure 10.6 shows how the awkward shapes created by the profile of the head and the contour of the shadows can be resolved by some slight adjustments.

10.4 WEAK PALETTE CHOICES

Quality palette choice is one of the key aspects to creating successful Pixel Art. Palette errors usually fall into the following categories:

- Too much or too little contrast (Figure 10.7)

FIGURE 10.7 Low contrast on the left, high contrast on the right.

- Too much or too little saturation (Figure 10.8)

FIGURE 10.8 High saturation on the left, low saturation or "muted" colors on the right.

- Too many colors (Figure 10.9)

FIGURE 10.9   A potentially problematic palette.

10.5 TOO MUCH COMPLEXITY

This one is my personal weakness and I fall into this making this mistake more often than I care to admit. Early on in a project I'll decide to create a sprite that looks really nice and not give much thought about the scope of the project; over time I'll notice all the places where the quality level will need to be raised to match that sprite. Before I know it, things have snowballed out of control. When I add more sprites into the project, I begin to notice the extensive palette choice I made; and when it's time to animate I inevitably regret that the first sprite was done elegantly. Why couldn't I have started with crap!? And really once a standard of quality has been set, it should be maintained throughout the entire process for the sake of consistency—and that can cause some major growing pains.

Besides, this is Pixel Art for goodness sake—it's *supposed* to be simple! Often times, players will actually prefer a simply aesthetic.

When you decide on your final aesthetic, consider your project scope and remember the acronym KISS: keep it simple, stupid.

10.6 FLASH SHADING

Sometimes people will shade in their images by making the edges of the object the darkest point and this can make the form appear flat. Often this is called pillow shading although I do not know why. But I call this flash shading because I think that this inclination comes from using flash photography for source images—as it somewhat emulates a light source similar to a photo taken with a flash like Figure 10.10.

This particular technique doesn't bother me nearly as much as it does some of my colleagues, many of which become violently ill to the point of projectile vomiting when they see "pillow shading."

Overall this technique gives a fairly mediocre result and seems particularly weak when compared to a more realistic light source like in Figure 10.11.

FIGURE 10.10   Boring "flash" shading.

FIGURE 10.11   Decent shading from an overhead light source.

10.7 NO TEXTURE

This is not an issue that is unique to Pixel Art, I see this particular oversight in the work of art students everywhere. When people start to learn how to use light and shadow to create form, there seems to be an almost universal amnesia that objects have texture.

An object will react to light differently depending on a number of different surface attributes that include transparency or translucence, reflectivity, and coarseness. Not to mention that the object may be more than one color, which would likely affect the value.

FIGURE 10.12   Surfaces have texture.

Take a look at the two mugs from Figure 10.12. The version on the left definitely implies form and gives a sense of depth but there is almost no texture implied in the drawing.

The wine glass on the left of Figure 10.13 suffers from the same affliction. You can see the top line of the liquid, so the viewer can tell that the glass has some translucency, but no other surface information is given about the glass. The wine glass on the right in contrast gives the viewer tons of information about the qualities of the material. There are many places where the purple color of the background is clearly visible through the glass, showing it's transparency. There are also places where there is implied reflection as well as specular highlights. Even the shadow that it casts gives information about the nature of the surface of the glass, showing that the glass has transparency as well as light that gets refracted.

FIGURE 10.13   Boring vs. interesting texture.

It may not be feasible to go into this level of detail when you create your Pixel Art, and that is okay. But it is important to know that these properties exist and can be conveyed within your imagery.

CHAPTER 11

Interviews with Game Developers

I HAVE SPOKEN AT LENGTH about the many virtuous and wonderful aspects of using Pixel Art but let's hear from some folks who are proactively using these techniques in the field. I've spoken with a couple of contemporary independent game developers about their choice to use Pixel Art in their projects

Although brief, their responses were not edited down and reflect the advantages and drawbacks candidly.

11.1 AN INTERVIEW WITH JAMES PETRUZZI OF DISCORD GAMES

FIGURE 11.1 Screenshot from Chasm.

I had the good fortune to speak with James Petruzzi of Discord games about their game Chasm.

Chasm is a beautiful looking 2D platform style game featuring dynamically generated dungeons. The game was funded through Kickstarter in May 2013 with 6938 backers (myself being one of them). And their game is particularly relevant to us because Chasm was built with hand-placed, jaw-dropping, awe-inspiring Pixel Art (Figures 11.1 through 11.4).

At the time of the writing of this book the game is still unreleased, so it is a real privilege to get this interview at this juncture in their busy schedule.

1. Why did you and your team choose to use Pixel Art for Chasm?

   I chose it for two reasons: the first is that it has a certain nostalgic quality that reminds me of the games I grew up with, and I really wanted to make something that looked like it could have existed on Super Nintendo when I was a kid. The second is that, like cartoons, it contains less detailed information about the world that allows the viewer to fill in the gaps with their imagination. I've found that the more detailed things are, the harder they are to sell as a simulation.

FIGURE 11.2   Screenshot from Chasm.

2. What advantages or disadvantage have there been using Pixel Art in your game?

A common misconception is that Pixel Art is less work than other styles, so it hasn't really saved us any time over, say, plain old digital art. It can also be a pain in our case since our native resolution is 384×216. Sometimes you want things to scroll smoother at smaller increments than is possible. When it comes down to it a pixel is either "here" or "there," not some place in between like with high-resolution displays. Things like player customization also factor in heavily. In 3D, it's much easier to have more variations, like layering equipment and such. This becomes very infeasible for fluid animated sprite characters since you need to hand make a variation for every possible frame.

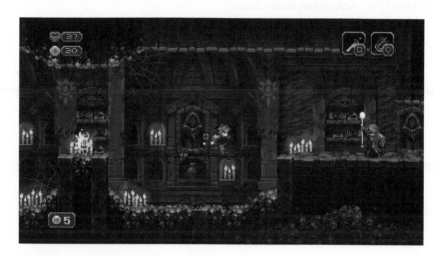

FIGURE 11.3   Screenshot from Chasm.

3. How have players responded to your game's aesthetic?

Players have responded to the art style better than we could have ever hoped. We took a big risk by not mixing resolutions or using gradients, ambient lighting, or other modern conveniences. We wanted something that looked as authentic as possible to a SNES or Genesis era title, and it seems to have paid off for us. As soon as someone sees the game they pretty much immediately "get it" if it's something they're interested in. It's certainly made selling the game much easier for us, as it basically tells the audience what it is just by the visual style.

FIGURE 11.4 Screenshot from Chasm.

Bonus point question: Do the artists on your team have any tips or techniques they'd like to share with us?

I will check with the artists and see if they have any tips.

Thanks for your time James!

Note: Unfortunately, their team has been very busy and hasn't been able to follow up with the tips that we all desire—but having this brief interview was a fantastic experience.

11.2 AN INTERVIEW WITH JOCHUM SKOGLUND OF CRACKSHELL

I had the good fortune to speak with Jochum Skoglund of Crackshell about their game Hammerwatch.

Hammerwatch is a top-down hack and slash game with tons of Pixel Art—style eye candy (Figures 11.5 through 11.7), featuring co-op gameplay and multiple character classes and difficulty levels. The game is currently available at www.hammerwatch.com or through Steam. I've played through it (albeit on the easiest difficulty level) and loved it—a very fun time by my assessment.

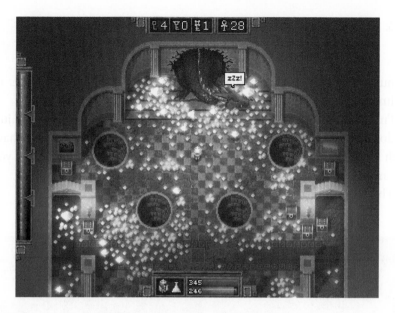

FIGURE 11.5 Screenshot from Hammerwatch.

1. Why did you choose to use Pixel Art for Hammerwatch?
   [It's] easier and faster than 3D.

2. What advantages or disadvantages have there been using Pixel Art in your game?
   2D isn't really effective when it comes to characters and such, when you need a great variety in equipments and so. Also, you need to draw each angle, you can't just rotate Pixel Art.

FIGURE 11.6 Screenshot from Hammerwatch.

3. How have players responded to your game's aesthetic?
We've had a great response on our graphics.

Bonus point question: Do the Artists on your team have any tips or techniques they'd like to share with us?

I'm the artist and this was my first Pixel Art ever, but I think if you just sit down and apply yourself, you'll get it after a while. Most issues artist have with Pixel Art seems to be angles of light, but it's not really that hard, you just need to think in 3D, but draw in 2D.

Thanks for the guidance Jochum!

FIGURE 11.7   Screenshot from Hammerwatch.

11.3 AN INTERVIEW WITH DAVE PRESTON OF HEART MACHINE

FIGURE 11.8   Screenshot from Hyper Light Drifter.

I had the pleasure to speak with Alex Preston of Heart Machine about their game Hyper Light Drifter.

Hyper Light Drifter is a gorgeous 2D Action RPG heavily influenced by early 8-bit and 16-bit games. The game was funded through Kickstarter in September of 2013 with 24,150 backers and raised significantly more cash than they hoped for. Hyper Light Drifter is being built using breathtaking Pixel Art (Figures 11.8 through 11.11) and we have this unique opportunity to find out more about their process.

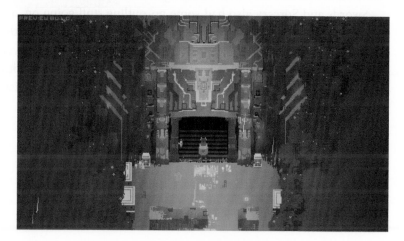

FIGURE 11.9   Screenshot from Hyper Light Drifter.

1. Why did you and your team choose Pixel Art for the game?

   I love the aesthetic and I grew up with blocky games. . . but it was originally a choice of efficiency. I had originally imagined creating the Art for the game in a high resolution, fully illustrative style but it became clear that it would just take too long. There were things that I wanted to do in the game that would have been impossible for a single person, at least with the variety that I needed. So Pixel Art just fit the bill for efficiency and it turned out to be more than that.

2. What advantages and disadvantages have there been using Pixel Art?

   Disadvantages: It was sometimes hard to express certain specific things like emotions because we have such a limited canvas size. It is also difficult to make rounded objects if we don't want them to look crumby.

   Advantages: The constraints allowed me to do a *lot* and focus on things that I wouldn't have been able to otherwise. I think it was the rigid structure has kept me in line. It allowed me to do creative things I wouldn't have thought of otherwise.

3. I noticed it doesn't seem like you use any outlines, which is kind of uncommon. Can you tell me about your decision to do that?

   There are a couple of examples of pixel style games that were being made without outlines before Hyper Light Drifter—and now everybody and their mother is doing it <chuckle>. Super Time Force was a good example. Also the guys from Capy—they have some fantastic artists and they were dabbling in that style before.

   Swords and Sorcery also had some no-outline stuff going on, and I think they really helped push it into popularity. Fez also did that to a degree. I was mostly inspired by that set of games that were mainstream-ish and able to really showcase what could be done without a thick black outline. Although my Art—my illustrative style—isn't really line work anyway.

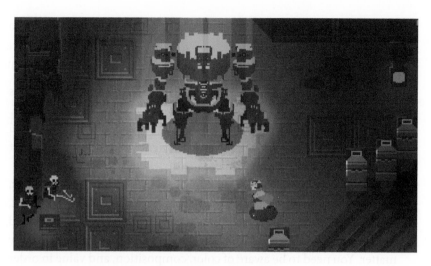

FIGURE 11.10   Screenshot from Hyper Light Drifter.

4. How have players responded to the aesthetic?

   Very positively. I am a very private person usually, so it was a very unusual thing for me to have such a public and intense reaction to what I'm working on.

   We got a lot of fan art from the Kickstarter launch and that felt crazy to me! It wasn't on my radar that people would react that way. I put the Art out there because I wanted to make the game... And to get all of that intense reaction to it—it was great! It is great.

5. Have you come across any surprises while creating Art for Hyper Light Drifter?

   This is the first time I've made a game at this scale with a team and I'm responsible for a lot of things. There are a lot of twists and turns in game development and there have been surprises all the time. There's a lot to figure out when making tiles or making enemy sprites. I'm not sure I could name one in particular because there are so many.

6. Are there any things that you built for Hyper Light Drifter that you are particularly proud of? Particular favorites?

   Building the whole game is kind of my favorite right now <chuckle>. If you need a specific example...there were some ninja frogs that I made recently that I really enjoy.

7. What single thing do you think makes the biggest difference in the success of a piece of Pixel Art?

I would say color choices.

8. Do you have any tips or techniques that would be helpful to the readers of the book?

The thing that's worked best when I'm doing any kind of Pixel Art—whether it be character or environment—is just being aware of everything that it's going to interact with.

This may be more true for our game because we don't have outlines. With solid colors it can be really challenging to make things pop out. I think just being aware of where the piece of Art is going to be placed in your game and the things around it because those associations really matter. You need to be aware of color, composition, and value in order for something to either blend in or stand out.

You can't design in a bubble.

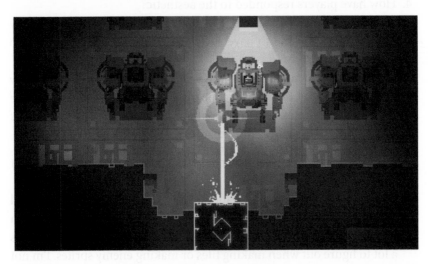

FIGURE 11.11   Screenshot from Hyper Light Drifter.

CHAPTER 12

Resources

D ON'T STOP YOUR GROWTH with the completion of this book! There are a number of fantastic resources for refining your abilities as a Pixel Artist. Following are a number of resources that I've found useful throughout my own journey as a game artist.

12.1 ONLINE RESOURCES

1. Pixelation—Way of the Pixel: http://wayofthepixel.net/
   An online Pixel Art forum with an emphasis on improving technique through critique.

2. Pixel Joint: http://www.pixeljoint.com/forum
   An online Pixel Art forum where there is more of an emphasis on the Pixel Art community.

3. Pixel Prospector—The indie goldmine: http://www.pixelprospector. com/ This is the motherload of links to articles, videos, tutorials, and other resources for game development.

12.2 BOOKS

1. *Drawing on the Right side of the Brain* by Betty Edwards
   The single most clever book I've read teaching how to draw, filled with ideas and exercises.

2. *The Animator's Survival Kit* by Richard Williams
   An incredible book for learning animation.

3. *Essentialism: The Disciplined Pursuit of Less* by Greg McKeown
Although not specifically linked to Pixel Art in any way, I cannot
endorse this book enough for task completion and generally improving quality of life.

12.3 PIXEL ART SOFTWARE

Although this is not a comprehensive list, I still have not had an opportunity
to use all of these programs listed. For that reason, I can't openly endorse all
of these. I'd suggest to try several and see what works for you. I've catego-
rized the list by operating system.

Windows:

- Aseprite

- GrafX2

- GraphicsGale

- mtPaint

- Pickle

- Pro Motion

- Pyxel Edit

- RagePixel (**Unity extension**)

- RotSprite

Mac:

- Aseprite

- GrafX2

- Pickle

- Pyxel Edit

- PikoPixel

- Pixen

- PXL
- RotSprite

Online:

- MakePixelArt: http://makepixelart.com/free/
- Piq: http://piq.codeus.net/draw
- Pxlr: http://apps.pixlr.com/editor/

CHAPTER 13

Afterword

Some Thoughts on Why I Wrote This Book

THERE ARE MANY THINGS I LOVE about working on games. I adore the marriage between creativity and problem solving. I actually love the surprises—the little idiosyncrasies where you think things are going to be easy and in fact they are not. I even enjoy the compromises that need to be made on a project in order to make a completed product.

So why did I spend the time to create this book rather than working on another game?

I have many passions but at some point the volume of my interests became a burden. I became a nervous wreck and felt buried under too many ideas, prototypes, and other commitments. After feeling somewhat crazed I found myself reading a book called *Essentialism: The Disciplined Pursuit of Less* by Greg McKeown and decided to shed my various interests and obligations down to one major project. I was committed not to start a single other project until I was finished with my number one priority.

But since I was dropping so many disparate interests simultaneously, I could not take my choice of projects lightly. I wanted to work on the one thing that could allow me to give my biggest contribution that I am capable at this juncture in time. What should it be? I had some interesting ideas for a 3D game—but was that a good idea given my skills and talents? Should I make a 2D game about monsters playing basketball? Team up with a friend to create a shmup? Write and promote a shred guitar album? A book on creative guitar soloing? I found myself with more questions than I started with.

Eventually, I decided to create a Venn diagram with three circles: One for things that I wanted to create, another that contained things that I am good at, and the last a list of things that I could create that would be helpful or likely to be wanted by other people. When framing my options through the lens of that diagram, it became obvious that a book on how to create Pixel Art was objectively the strongest contribution that I could offer at this juncture in time.

Thank you for reading this, I hope that you were able to get some useful ideas from the book. I ended up learning a lot through the process—more than I would have expected.

Best of luck and perhaps we can chat on one of the Pixel Art forums online or at the Game Developers Conference sometime!

Also be sure to join my mailing list at www.learnpixelart.com

Index

Printed and bound by CPI Group (UK) Ltd, Croydon, CR0 4YY

21/10/2024

01777108-0003